KITCHENS OF HOPE

Immigrants Share Stories of Resilience and Recipes from Home

KITCHENS OF HOPE

Immigrants Share Stories of Resilience and Recipes from Home

Linda S. Svitak and Christin Jaye Eaton
with Lee Svitak Dean

Foreword by Loan Huynh · Photography by Tom Wallace

UNIVERSITY OF MINNESOTA PRESS
MINNEAPOLIS
LONDON

The University of Minnesota Press gratefully acknowledges assistance provided for the publication of this book by the John K. and Elsie Lampert Fesler Fund.

For the sake of uniformity, the recipes have been standardized to the style common in U.S. cookbooks.

Quotation on p. vi from Michelle T. King, *Chop Fry Watch Learn: Fu Pei-mei and the Making of Modern Chinese Food* (New York: W.W. Norton & Company, Inc., 2024).

Published by the University of Minnesota Press
111 Third Avenue South, Suite 290
Minneapolis, MN 55401–2520
http://www.upress.umn.edu

ISBN 978-1-5179-1912-2 (hc)
ISBN 978-1-5179-1913-9 (pb)

A Cataloging-in-Publication record for this book is available from the Library of Congress.

Printed in Canada on acid-free paper

33 32 31 30 29 28 27 26 10 9 8 7 6 5 4 3 2

To all those who have traveled great distances in search of better lives

Across the street from my office in Washington, D.C., is the National Archives, and there are the documents of the creation of our country. You can read the whole thing, the Declaration of Independence, the Bill of Rights. But when you go and you read those three words, "We the People," if you keep repeating "We the People, We the People, We the People, We the People," you learn that these are three very important words. Everyone should remember that "We the People" is who we are as Americans. All the people. A nation of inclusion, not exclusion.

—José Andrés, immigrant, chef, humanitarian

• • • •

Cuisine cannot exist without the free and fair movement of ingredients, ideas, and people. Deliciousness is an undeniable benefit of immigration. When people move around, food gets better.

—Chris Ying, editor of *You and I Eat the Same: On the Countless Ways Food and Cooking Connect Us to One Another*

• • • •

Food is eminently portable. If the memory of a dish lingers on your tongue and you know how to cook the dishes of your family, the taste of home is never farther than your kitchen, wherever you have landed in life.

—Michelle T. King, author of *Chop Fry Watch Learn: Fu Pei-mei and the Making of Modern Chinese Food*

CONTENTS

FOREWORD

THE POWER OF ONE

Loan Huynh

I believe in the power of one: each of us individually has the potential to make an indelible difference in the lives of those around us and for many generations. One man, a captain of a ship, made the decision to pick up my family along the beaches of Saigon on April 30, 1975, when the city fell to the North Vietnamese troops.

I was five years old. My three siblings; my Ba (father); my Me (mother), who was nine months pregnant with my brother; and I, along with other family members and some of my father's military troop who loyally stayed with him, had driven along the beaches of Saigon to find a way to escape Vietnam.

All the ships were out in the harbor or at sea. My Ba waved his white T-shirt and begged for one of the nearby ships to come back to get his children, even if they could not take him and my Me. The captain saw us, my parents and their four little children, ages six years old and younger, and he sent a boat to pick us up to transport us to the ship, which was already fully loaded with passengers. This captain's single decision saved our lives, as my Ba was in counterintelligence for South Vietnam, and there was no doubt he would have been killed if he was unable to escape.

My Ba and the ship captain remained lifelong friends. Many years later, when my Ba made his annual phone call in April to thank his friend, he asked the captain what made him come back to pick us up. The captain said he was moved to help when he saw my Ba's four children and heard his plea to take us without our parents.

Today, one of my sisters is a James Beard award–winning journalist, one of my brothers owns a restaurant and bar that employs dozens of people, another sister became a child therapist and helps immigrants, and the baby brother born in the refugee camp of Fort Chaffee, Arkansas, is an alumnus of Harvard University and an award-winning political consultant. For me, I lived my dream of becoming a human rights and immigration lawyer, along with being the mother of two beautiful girls who are first-generation Americans.

I hope our captain knows the ripple effect he initiated—his own power of one. I do, as we gather around my parents' dining table in Houston for my Me's *pho* each Christmas Eve. I am forever grateful.

••••

The story of my family, like that of so many other immigrants, speaks from experience. Regardless of the reasons or the events that draw us to the United States, once here we build communities that inevitably revolve around food, and not only for those around our tables but also for friends, neighbors, and others who want to explore the flavors of our heritage. Hear our stories in the pages of *Kitchens of Hope*, including my Me's recipe for *pho*.

INTRODUCTION
THE IMPORTANCE OF STORIES

They packed little but memories as they headed to the United States. For immigrants trying to fit a lifetime into a suitcase, there wasn't much room. They carried with them thoughts of home. Of family and friends. Of the aroma of cardamom, the tang of fish sauce, the heat of chile peppers, the bite of mustard greens. As they rebuilt their lives in the United States, many in Minnesota, they turned to the familiar comfort foods and traditions that lingered in their hearts, minds, and palates. Curry and *mole*. *Biryani* and borscht. Pita and *pho*. *Sambusas* and *pupusas*. Together, this wealth of flavors and fragrances would ignite their senses and expand the world for their new friends and neighbors.

This book originated as an effort to collect the mealtime memories—the recipes—of those who had left their home countries behind for life in the United States. As we began collecting recipes, though, we recognized that the stories behind the cooks were as compelling as the brimming bowls and overflowing platters that represented their culinary treasures.

These stories offered more than the stark numbers that often define the migration of people from one country to another: the visas and green cards, the countries and populations. That familiar bare-bones approach overlooks the lives of those on the move. Simply ask the families who fled the collapse of Saigon decades ago. Or those from war-torn Somalia or the political turmoil of Democratic Republic of Congo, among the many terrors of the modern world. Others have made their journeys not out of fear but for the sake of opportunity, be it education, business, family, or other reasons. They, too, carry stories.

The narratives in this cookbook speak of the lives of everyday people, the courageous who left the familiar and journeyed great distances for something better. Those featured here come from Afghanistan to Zimbabwe, representing more than thirty countries on the world map.

••••

Every recipe tells a story, and those in this collection are no exception. As one interview after another progressed, what surprised us was the enthusiasm that the storytelling prompted. "When is *our* book coming out?" asked many who were profiled, delighted not only to tell their stories but also to be heard.

"I would like to meet this person I'm reading about," says one who was featured, about her own narrative.

"Be open-minded about new foods," suggests a participant.

"This recipe reminds me of home," comments another.

"Food is our cultural DNA," describes a cook. "Food tells our story."

Indeed, it does, which is why this framework of recipes-plus-stories made sense to us. As the cooks chopped onions and peppers, boiled chicken and cooked rice, we stood nearby taking notes, occasionally helping with the prep work. As the fragrance of home cooking wafted through the kitchen, the participants explained the process behind the culinary rituals before us. We served as transcribers and tasters, with contributors approving the rendition of their lives provided here.

And we took photographs, so many photographs, of the people and the food they prepared. Some immigrants preferred not to appear visually in the book; some had changed their names for reasons of privacy or for concern of violence toward family overseas. These are the real-life concerns that some immigrants face. For these reasons, we intentionally avoided including the names of most family members of those we interviewed, unless we were specifically asked to include them.

As we gathered the stories, what surprised us were the tales behind many personal histories of people we had known for years, details that were never mentioned in the day-to-day exchanges with friends, neighbors, and colleagues. This made us understand the truth that hides in all personal interactions. Everyone has a tale to tell, and it likely isn't what others expect, or hear, during a casual conversation. Our life stays in the dark until someone suggests, "Tell me your story."

And that's what we did.

••••

The recipes in this book, tested in home kitchens, are delightful and doable, regardless of the expertise of whoever is doing the cooking. Most of the ingredients are available in supermarkets, with some found only at specialty grocery stores or through online shopping. Not familiar with *ají panca*, a mild Peruvian pepper? How about Maggi seasoning, or tamarind fruit, or *palaw* spices from Afghanistan? Thirty-seven very proud cooks hope you will give these flavors a try.

••••

The volume in your hands does not look like most cookbooks. *Kitchens of Hope* does not have typical chapters that take the reader from appetizers to main dishes to desserts. Instead, the sections of this cookbook are inspired by elements of the stories that are told: ones that reflect community, resilience, opportunity, justice, hope, and celebration. While all the stories echo these attributes to different degrees, each one profiles how food and family are woven into the fabric of immigrants' lives as they adapt to a new world. The portrayals include a favorite recipe or two from each cook, often a comfort food brought from a home country—a gift to the reader—that also recalls kitchen fragrances, open-air markets, and neighbors who stop by for a meal. These recipes serve as road maps of homes that people have left and journeys that they have taken.

Meet these remarkable women and men in *Kitchens of Hope*, people who took leaps of faith, uprooted their families or themselves, persevered at great effort, all to begin new lives in the United States. They are our neighbors, our colleagues, our friends, and they have generously given readers a peek into their lives and kitchens. They invite you to break bread with them.

Welcome to the *Kitchens of Hope* table.

••••

The authors' proceeds from this book will benefit the Advocates for Human Rights, a global nonprofit organization based in Minnesota that provides free legal help to those seeking asylum, to those in immigration detention, to unaccompanied children, and for other human rights issues.

THE ADVOCATES FOR HUMAN RIGHTS

In 1983, a group of Minnesota lawyers believed that the community's spirit of social justice and volunteerism was an opportunity to improve human rights conditions worldwide. They created the Advocates for Human Rights, an independent, nonprofit, nongovernmental organization dedicated to the promotion and protection of internationally recognized human rights.

The Advocates for Human Rights believes everyone has the power to advance human rights. By engaging nearly 1,500 volunteers in hands-on human rights work each year, this organization accomplishes critical research and advocacy, transforming volunteers into advocates for human rights.

With a focus on systemic change and direct services, the Advocates for Human Rights grounds its policy work in real-life experiences, bridging the gap between advocacy and action. When clients experience injustice, the Advocates helps them and works to change the systems that perpetuate those injustices. When partners report barriers to safety and security, the Advocates identifies the gaps in legal protections and develops solutions.

Rooted in deep expertise and strong relationships, the Advocates collaborates in partnerships in its home community and around the globe to address some of the world's most intractable human rights issues. This work includes:

- partnering with legal professionals in thousands of cases annually to help people navigate complex immigration proceedings if they are seeking asylum from persecution or torture; survivors of human trafficking; unaccompanied children; and people detained by U.S. Immigration and Customs Enforcement (ICE).
- mobilizing volunteers to strengthen transparency and accountability by monitoring hearings in federal immigration court and in state cases involving gender-based violence.
- partnering with human rights defenders worldwide to hold governments accountable for human rights violations through advocacy at the United Nations.
- convening Global Women's Watch, a coalition of women's human rights defenders from more than twenty countries united in fighting the antigender movement.
- supporting the right to education through the Sankhu Palubari Community School in Nepal.

Learn more at www.theadvocatesforhumanrights.org.

The Advocates
FOR HUMAN RIGHTS

KITCHENS OF COMMUNITY

We all need community, especially when our lives are disrupted. Comfort often comes through feeding those around us or receiving such a meal. Doris Parker left her home in Liberia to escape a war, and today cooks with ingredients from local African grocery stores and farmers markets. José Alarcon brought his family's tradition of shared meals from his childhood home in Mexico to restaurants in Minneapolis and beyond. Nadya Goncharova left Latvia to broaden her world and discovered a like-minded wilderness in northern Minnesota and a career in hospitality. Jesus Li, who traveled from Peru to Minnesota for partnership and education, found that food builds community. Gus and Kate Romero blended their heritage (Mexican and Polish) to create their own culinary world. Emilia Olabisi Fatmata Smith lived through war in Sierra Leone, until her father brought their family to Minnesota. The deeper meaning of food—that it's meant to be shared—has stayed the same. They all found community, and their way home, in the kitchen.

DORIS PARKER

LIBERIA

Faded Polaroid photographs made all the difference. After two civil wars in Liberia, Doris Parker's family had dispersed, their house had burned down, and the family records were destroyed. She had to find a way to prove the family relationships necessary to apply for a sibling petition to live in the United States. She showed the officials two photographs of her family, taken decades earlier. The pictures made the connection and, in 2010, after years in limbo, Doris received her green card (permanent residency to live and work in the United States).

One photograph was taken in 1982 in Liberia. The other was taken sixteen years later in the United States with almost all the same members present. "That's all it took to convince immigration that we were family," says Doris.

She was born in Monrovia, the capital of Liberia, in West Africa, and grew up in Roberts Field. Doris graduated from high school in 1983, coming to the United States three years later after an attempted coup in Liberia, but before the war broke out. Fearing for her safety, her father had wanted Doris to join her two siblings and cousins who were already in the United States. She left

Doris Parker

for there, while the rest of her family stayed behind. When war broke out in 1990, her family scattered, her father and remaining siblings fleeing to a refugee camp in Sierra Leone, while other relatives headed to Côte d'Ivoire and Guinea. One sister was captured and went missing for twelve years.

The immigration process was a struggle. Doris had a temporary status for years, despite pursuing multiple avenues to seek asylum. She qualified for political asylum based on her tribal affiliation, but the application remained pending. She applied through Temporary Protected Status, Deferred Enforced Departure, and Diversity Lottery, each with its own requirements and timetable. At times she represented herself and, on other occasions, a lawyer assisted. Looking back, Doris says she is humbled by the challenges. "Sometimes when you face hard times, it makes you a better person."

She did not let her temporary status hold her back. She attended St. Catherine University in St. Paul, obtained a nursing degree, and began to work. She bought a home and built a life in Minnesota and continued to contribute to her country—both of them.

As the wars in Liberia wound down, Doris observed the influx of Liberian young people coming from refugee camps to settle in the Twin Cities, traumatized by what they had seen and by the loss of their parents. They had missed school for years. As there was no support in place to assist these refugees as they acclimated to their new environment, Doris helped found the Liberian Women's Initiative in 2003. This was a group of women committed to tackling the problems they saw: education, teen pregnancy, dropping out of high-school. The Initiative instituted mentoring and after-school programs to help young Liberian women transition into new homes in a new country.

Equally important, the Liberian Truth and Reconciliation Commission was established by the country's parliament to address the causes of, and crimes committed during, the civil wars. Doris worked with the Advocates for Human Rights on ways to engage the local Liberian community to support the commission's fact-finding mission. Liberians were reluctant to share their stories, as the memories were painful and they feared retaliation by perpetrators who were still free. Doris testified to the commission from the United States on behalf of her sister who had been held hostage, and who still lives in Liberia.

Doris returned to Liberia in 2014, after almost three decades in the United States, to help combat the Ebola epidemic. An experienced nurse, she was one of six volunteers from Minnesota who underwent training by the Centers for Disease Control and Prevention and the U.S. Department of Defense on care related to the disease. She spent three months working with patients in rural Liberia, at times wearing a hazmat suit in extreme heat.

Doris has lived her entire adult life in the United States. "This is home," she says. "We love this country, and I feel like I can contribute to American society." But Liberia is a part of her, and food is an important part of that connection. She recalls struggling to find ingredients for Liberian foods when she first came to the United States in the 1980s. She used mashed potato instead of cassava to make *fufu*. Today, there are a number of African grocery stores that carry Liberian specialties, but she finds the farmers markets the most exciting and interesting places to shop.

"Hmong, Asians, and Africans grow ingredients and it's so surprising. How did *kitily* [a type of eggplant] and *palava* greens [jute leaves] grow in Minnesota?" she wonders. Look for the ingredients for her recipes, peanut soup and Liberian rice bread, at a nearby farmers market or local African grocery store. The recipe for the rice bread is from Doris's sister, Cora Parker, who lives in Minneapolis.

Peanut Soup

Peanut Soup

Makes 6 to 7 cups

- 1 medium tomato
- 2 red bell peppers
- 2 onions, roughly chopped
- 1 Maggi cube or vegetable bouillon cube, dissolved in 1 cup water (see Note)
- ½ teaspoon freshly ground black pepper
- ½ teaspoon cayenne pepper, optional
- ½ cup creamy-style natural peanut butter
- Red pepper, chopped peanuts, and chopped parsley, for garnish

NOTE: Maggi seasoning comes in liquid, cube, and powdered forms. It enhances food with a deep, umami-rich flavor.

Bring a large pot of water to boil over high heat. Carefully drop the tomato in the boiling water for 30 to 60 seconds, then remove and place it on a cutting board until it is cool enough to handle. Repeat with the bell peppers.

Rub the skin off the tomato and core the tomato. Discard the peppers' stems and seeds. In a blender, combine the tomato, bell peppers, onions, and dissolved Maggi (or bouillon) cube and process until smooth.

In a medium saucepan over medium heat, combine the vegetable purée, black pepper, and cayenne pepper (optional). If the mixture is too thick, add a bit more water.

In a medium bowl, mix the peanut butter gradually into 2 cups water. Add the peanut butter mixture to the soup and cook, stirring occasionally, until heated through. Add more water to adjust consistency. Serve hot. Garnish, if desired.

Doris and her family

Cora Parker's Liberian Rice Bread

Makes one pan (about 24 bars)

Rice bread is a staple in Liberia that can serve as either a dessert or an appetizer.

Butter or vegetable oil for greasing pan

2¼ cups (14 ounces) Cream of Rice cereal (see Note)

½ cup granulated sugar

2 teaspoons baking soda

1 teaspoon baking powder

½ teaspoon nutmeg or 1 teaspoon ground ginger

½ teaspoon salt

8 large or 10 small bananas, very ripe

1 cup milk

2 eggs

1 cup vegetable oil

Preheat the oven to 350°F. Grease the bottom and sides of a 9- by 13-inch pan with butter or vegetable oil.

In a medium bowl, combine the dry rice cereal, sugar, baking soda, baking powder, nutmeg (or ginger), and salt. Set aside.

In the bowl of an electric mixer, mash the bananas. Add the milk, eggs, and 1 cup vegetable oil, and beat on medium speed until thoroughly incorporated.

Reduce the speed to low and add the cereal mixture in two parts, mixing until thoroughly incorporated and smooth. Pour the batter into the prepared baking pan and bake until brown (the color of banana bread), about 45 to 60 minutes. Remove from the oven and transfer the baking pan to a wire rack to cool for at least 20 minutes.

NOTE: Some cooks prefer more (or less) banana in this bread. This could also be made in two (4- by 9-inch) loaf pans. The batter is very thin. This recipe uses a granular rice cereal, such as Cream of Rice.

Cora Parker

JOSÉ ALARCON

MEXICO

José Alarcon

As a child in Morelos, Mexico, José Alarcon rose at dawn to carry baked goods in a basket perched atop his head while walking or riding his bike up and down hills to the market where his grandparents sold those items. In his small town, most people did not have refrigerators, so residents would go to the market and get only enough food for the day. Vendors set out their onions, tomatoes, cilantro, *papalo* leaves, herbs, and many snacks made from masa, a corn dough that, when cooked on a griddle, produced a memorable aroma.

Later, as an adult in Minneapolis, José was the chef behind three restaurants: Popul Vuh, for fine dining; Centro, a fast-casual *taquería*; and Vivir, a cafe, market, and bakery. All three served foods inspired by the fragrances of the Mexican market from his childhood.

Central to José's journey has been his passion to learn. He was fifteen years old when his father passed away. José wanted to help support his mother, his younger sister, and his brother in any way he could, which was in line with the expectation in his culture

that the oldest child would take care of the family. After he finished high school, following the example of many people who went before, José came to the United States to earn money he could send back to his family. At the age of eighteen, he says, "I thought 'I can do anything.'"

He needed this can-do spirit, as he came to the United States not speaking any English. He knew he had to learn the language to be able to communicate, "to have that freedom," he says. When not too busy working, José went to the library and found books to teach him English. He also went to a school that taught English as a Second Language to adults. Early in his time in the United States, José needed to take two buses to get to his job as a dishwasher. Sometimes, when he had extra time waiting for the second bus, he would go inside a bookstore to keep warm and look at books. At first, he only paged through the volumes to pass the time. That shifted to studying books to understand how to work more efficiently in a professional kitchen.

José began searching for new ideas about how to prepare, cook, and sell food. His knowledge came from magazines, books, and people, joining up with teams at many different restaurants. "At that point," José recalls, "I was so into cooking and trying to learn. I learned as much as I can wherever I worked. My driving emotion was to show up and learn."

José knew he wanted to open a restaurant if he got the opportunity, but he didn't know what kind of food he would cook. Initially, he didn't think of cooking what he grew up eating. That changed when he took a break from fine dining restaurants and worked as a butcher, which gave him time to think over possibilities. That led to him wanting to focus on Mexican food if he had the chance. His cooking now incorporates many flavors he recalls from his childhood, though he doesn't have many recipes from that time, as he grew up eating, not cooking.

"When you're eating, you remember the context as well as the food," José says. "At the end of the day you want people to have a good meal, but also really good service too. That means the place should feel welcoming, like home."

Every day in Mexico, people sit down with family for lunch and dinner. And those family gatherings are big in Mexico. For Christmas, at least twenty-five people would gather at José's grandparents' house for a meal. There could be a roasted chicken, or *bacalao*, a very popular dish of cod fish cured in salt, with a side of beans and chiles.

José has been in the United States for nineteen years and recently celebrated his grant of citizenship. He loves the colder weather and even rides his bike in the snow. José says he feels privileged to have the opportunity now to travel back and forth to Mexico to see his family. And his community only keeps growing, as he meets new people and continues to learn about their culture and their food.

"I'm always learning," José says. "Never stop."

The classic Christmas meal in Mexico is *pozole*, which is sometimes made with hominy in the United States. In Mexico, nixtamalized corn is used. The ingredients vary by the region of Mexico. The dish is often served with pork or chicken and topped with an array of fixings (cabbage, cilantro, onions, as shown here). It can also be made as a broth without meat.

"But if you give it to a person from Mexico, they will say 'Where's my meat?'" José says.

Pozole Rojo (Red Pozole)

Serves 8 to 10

NOTE: Plan ahead, as the dried hominy must be soaked overnight. This can be made with either chicken or pork. Both the hominy and dried chile peppers can be found in Mexican grocery stores.

POZOLE

- 1 pound dried hominy (must be soaked overnight)
- 1 white onion, peeled and trimmed, left whole
- 10 garlic cloves, peeled and left whole
- 6 bay leaves
- 5 sprigs fresh thyme
- 3 tablespoons fresh oregano
- 2 to 3 pounds chicken breast, bone-in with skin, or 2 to 4 pounds pork shoulder or rib
- 2 tablespoons salt

TO MAKE THE HOMINY: Soak the kernels overnight in 3 to 4 cups water, then drain and rinse the corn. Put it in a pot with 4 cups of fresh water and bring to a boil over high heat. Reduce the heat to low and simmer, stirring occasionally, until tender, about 30 minutes. Add more water as needed. When done, drain any excess water and set aside.

TO MAKE THE BROTH: In a large pot, combine 1 onion, garlic, bay leaves, thyme, 3 tablespoons oregano, chicken or pork, and 2 tablespoons salt. Add 3 quarts (12 cups) water. Bring to a boil over high heat and cook for 3 minutes. Reduce the heat to low and simmer, uncovered, until the meat is tender, stirring occasionally. If using chicken, the meat will be done in about 20 to 25 minutes. If using pork, cook for about 2 hours. Add more water, if necessary, through the cooking process. While the meat cooks, skim off the foam and fat. When the meat is cooked, remove it from the broth and allow it to cool. Set the broth aside.

(recipe and ingredients continue on page 11)

Pozole Rojo

CHILE PURÉE

5 dried guajillo chile peppers

4 dried ancho chile peppers (a dried poblano pepper)

2 dried morita chile peppers (a type of chipotle pepper, like a red jalapeño)

2 dried árbol chiles (or use ½ to 1 chile for medium heat; omit altogether for milder heat)

1 teaspoon fresh oregano

½ teaspoon ground cumin

2 tablespoons vegetable oil

Salt, to taste

GARNISHES

½ small head green cabbage, or 1 Napa cabbage, finely chopped

½ white onion, finely chopped

3 limes, cut into quarters

2 avocados, peeled and cut into cubes

Freshly ground chile piquín (hotter than a jalapeño)

2 tablespoons fresh oregano

4 radishes, sliced

TO MAKE THE CHILE PURÉE: Remove the stem ends and seeds from the dried chiles. Toast the chiles in batches of about three peppers at a time on a hot *comal* (a dry skillet) or griddle, pressing down with a wooden spoon or tongs, for about 15 seconds on each side. Place all the chiles together in a medium-sized mixing bowl with hot water to cover (about 3 cups) and let sit for 10 to 15 minutes to hydrate the chiles.

Put the chiles with the water in a blender. Add 1 teaspoon oregano and ½ teaspoon cumin and process until smooth. Heat the oil in a pan, add the chile purée and salt to taste, and cook the mixture for about 5 minutes. Remove from the heat.

TO FINISH THE MEAT: Once the meat is cool, separate the meat from the skin and bones, discarding the skin and bones. Cut or shred the meat into generous bite-sized pieces. Your hands are a great "tool" for shredding chicken—you may wish to wear disposable kitchen gloves. Set the meat pieces aside. Strain and set the broth aside.

TO FINISH THE SOUP: Add the chile purée to the broth and bring to a boil over medium-high heat. Add the meat and cook for 10 minutes, then add the hominy and heat through.

TO SERVE: Place the pot of pozole on the table with all the garnishes in separate bowls. Let everyone dish up their own pozole and add their preferred garnishes.

dried hominy

NADYA GONCHAROVA
LATVIA

When someone asks Nadya Goncharova where she is from, there's a slight pause before she answers. It's complicated.

She was born in 1977 in Ukraine, in Crimea. At the time, Ukraine was part of the Soviet Union. Soon after, the government asked her parents, both civil engineers, to move to Latvia, where their expertise was needed. So, her family of three packed their bags and relocated. "It was beautiful, on the Baltic Sea, with forest and lots of things to do outdoors," Nadya says. "It was a happy childhood." A sister joined the family. By the time Nadya reached high school, Mikhail Gorbachev was leading the Soviet Union and the future seemed precarious. Her parents sent her alone on a train to live with her grandparents in Crimea to finish her last year of school.

When the Soviet Union collapsed in 1991, both of her parents lost their jobs. Nadya returned to the family home in Latvia to go to university, where she earned a five-year degree in business law. "The economics were so bad," she says. "In one day, all our family savings were gone." Making life more difficult, her family was legally without a country. "When Latvia became its own country,

Nadya Goncharova

those born in Latvia became citizens," she says. "But that didn't include us, who were born elsewhere."

Nadya hadn't yet planned what she would do after graduation when a classmate told her about a program in the United States where she could work and travel while living with an American family for a year and taking care of their children. Nadya thought it sounded impossible, but she enrolled and within weeks she had a job in Boston caring for grade-school children. Her parents were shocked. "I lived with an amazing family in Boston," she says. "They took me everywhere. They asked me where I wanted to study [as part of the *au pair* program] and I said 'Harvard,' and they enrolled me in a business class for one semester."

As her year with the family came to an end, Nadya visited a friend in northern Minnesota who was working at a resort in Tofte, on Lake Superior's North Shore. "I could not believe it. It was like Latvia," she says about both the wilderness and the inland sea within reach of the small town. Her Boston hosts urged her to stay in the United States, though her parents wanted her back in Latvia. "I decided to go where my heart was," she says. "I bought a ticket and came to northern Minnesota, where I had friends working hard and having dreams. There was nothing to go back to in Latvia. There were no jobs there, and my friends had movedaway."

Nadya enrolled at the University of Wisconsin in Superior, to complete a degree in the United States, in addition to her degree in Latvia. The university had a large English as a Second Language program and many international students. "It was the hardest experience of my life," she says. "I had to be on the same level with others, be fluent in writing. There were many sleepless nights and tears, but I graduated with high achievement. I had survival skills and was on a mission."

Nadya moved to Tofte and began a hospitality career. She mentored international students, many in the United States for the first time with big dreams and aspirations. After fifteen years working in restaurant management, where she had risen to food and beverage manager, she reached a crossroads. Approaching the age of forty and feeling ambitious, she wanted a change. She accepted a position with Culinaire International, which ran the dining offerings at the Walker Art Center in Minneapolis and elsewhere. After a few years working at the Walker, she moved to another Culinaire location, at the American Swedish Institute. There, she directs food and beverage for events and for the restaurant Fika. "Nothing was happening to me until I stepped out of my comfort zone, from Latvia, to Boston, to northern Minnesota, to Minneapolis. I feel blessed and so appreciative of the opportunities along the way," says Nadya, who is now a U.S. citizen. "That little piece of paper gave me satisfaction." Which is not to say there were no sacrifices. "I didn't see my parents for nine years."

Hospitality continues to be Nadya's driving force. "When you bring together people who are passionate, it's like magic. I can't get enough of it," Nadya says. Her recipe for walnut cake dates back to before her parents' wedding in Ukraine. "It's my great-aunt's cake, and she made it for two hundred people for the wedding," she says. "Since then, my mom was so proud of the cake that she made it for every holiday and birthday." The amount of walnuts used in the cake is determined by the baker. As a child, Nadya and her sister had to shell the walnuts their mother purchased. "We used fewer walnuts then," she says. "Now I buy them shelled at the grocery store."

Walnut Cake

Walnut Cake

Makes 1 (9-inch) layered cake; serves 10 to 12

- 2 cups chopped walnuts (see Note)
- 2 eggs, separated
- 1 cup granulated sugar
- 1½ cups flour
- 1 (14-ounce) can sweetened condensed milk, divided (see Note)
- 1 teaspoon baking soda
- 1 tablespoon white vinegar
- 1 cup (2 sticks) butter, at room temperature, plus more to grease the pan

NOTE: The quantity of walnuts will depend on how the cake is frosted and how many walnuts are preferred for decoration. The quantity listed here in this recipe will cover the filling and the top of the cake. One can of sweetened condensed milk is sufficient in total for making the cake and for the filling between the layers. You may need a second can of sweetened condensed milk, as well as additional butter, if you are frosting the entire exterior of the cake.

TO PREPARE THE WALNUTS: Preheat the oven to 350°F. Arrange the walnuts in a single layer on a baking sheet and toast them in the oven for 5 to 8 minutes. Remove the baking sheet from the oven, transfer the walnuts to a plate, and cool completely. Finely chop the walnuts.

TO MAKE THE CAKE: Grease the bottom and sides of a 9-inch round cake pan with butter. Beat the egg whites and sugar in the bowl of an electric mixer on medium-high speed until creamy, about 1 minute. Add the egg yolks and beat until thoroughly combined. Reduce the speed to low, add the flour and half (7 ounces) of the sweetened condensed milk, and mix until creamy.

Put the baking soda and vinegar in a small bowl and stir until the baking soda is dissolved. Stir the vinegar mixture into the cake batter. Pour the batter into the prepared baking pan and bake until golden brown and fully cooked on the inside (use a toothpick to check), about 30 minutes. Remove the cake from the oven and set it on a wire rack to cool to room temperature.

TO MAKE THE FROSTING: In the bowl of an electric mixer, combine the butter and the remaining sweetened condensed milk, and beat on medium speed until smooth.

TO ASSEMBLE THE CAKE: Cut the cooled cake in half horizontally. Use a spatula to spread half of the frosting on top of the bottom layer. Put one-fourth to one-half of the toasted walnuts on top of the frosting, then place the other half of the cake on top. Use a spatula to spread the remaining frosting on the top of the cake. Scatter the remaining walnuts on top of the frosting. To frost the sides of the cake, prepare additional frosting and use additional walnuts for decoration.

JESUS LI

PERU

After living for more than thirty years in Lima, Peru, Jesus Li faced a choice: stay in Lima or move to Minneapolis, where his partner had been accepted in a master's program. Lima was the safe option: Jesus had family and friends there and a good job as a graphic designer. A move to Minneapolis seemed risky. He knew nothing about the city except that it was in the middle of the United States, that it was cold, and that it was associated with the death of George Floyd.

Initially, Jesus was concerned that he wouldn't be able to find a job, that his writing and English skills weren't good enough, and that he wouldn't fit in. But he also understood that he did not have to replicate his current life. Instead, he had the power to shape his space, whether that was in Lima or in another country. His decision: leave Lima, apply to a master of fine arts program at the Minneapolis College of Art and Design (MCAD), and move to Minneapolis.

His first year in the city was hard and Jesus felt unmoored: "When you don't see recognizable icons or symbols that connect you to your culture,

Jesus Li

you can lose a sense of who you are," he says. "There were no Peruvian restaurants, no Peruvians around, nothing that might identify you as Peruvian." Even looking to the broader Latino community, Jesus observed that the focus was on Central America and the experience of crossing the border. But for those from various parts of South America, the immigrant experiences were very different.

Jesus became empowered by MCAD and the community he found there, including a mentor in Nancy Rice, a founder of Fallon Rice advertising agency. Those events inspired him to begin questioning what it means to belong. How does a Peruvian moving to Minneapolis "fit in" while maintaining his identity? How does relocating shape lives? As an MFA student, he searched for answers both academically and artistically. He studied precolonial influences and icons that reflect culture and identity, and then redesigned them into posters about Peruvian dances, a vital part of Peru's national identity. Jesus prepared his poster installation so that you do not simply observe the posters, but you must walk around them. You don't just see the dance; you dance with the poster.

As Jesus considered his own experience, he wondered whether other Latinos had similar experiences. He broadened his research to look at identity and cultural challenges that South Americans face when they move to Minneapolis. He interviewed individuals from other parts of South America—Colombia, Ecuador, Paraguay. He completed his thesis as part of his master's program, translating key words and concepts into artwork for a public show in 2023.

Jesus sees his research making a huge impact toward fostering diversity. He wants to understand what helps immigrants feel that they belong. This is far more than exchanging simple greetings and welcomes. The goal is to help people reach their potential.

Community is a critical part of belonging. "Food builds community," Jesus says. Growing up in Lima, he was particularly close to his grandmother, and was fascinated by her approach to cooking. She didn't have a book of recipes or sets of measurements. She cooked through the senses—what do you see, how does it taste, how does it smell? "I would try to sneak into the kitchen to watch her, peeking in the pots until she would tell me to go out of the kitchen," he says. "Cooking was hers. What she had in the kitchen was the power of cooking, of feeding people."

Jesus' recipe is for *Ají de Pollo*, a dish that was brought from Spain during the colonial period in Peru and has since been adapted. "Peruvians shape everything to our flavor," Jesus says. This dish took him years to learn, with his grandmother showing him one step at a time. She cooked this dish for him when she wanted to please him, when he got a good grade at school, or when he helped with chores. It was her way of showing affection. And Jesus now offers the same. The recipe that follows has instructions in the form he learned, using his senses.

Ají de Pollo (Peruvian Chicken)

Serves 6

NOTE: Plan ahead to hard-cook the eggs in advance. Order *ají amarillo* and *ají panca* online; both are Peruvian pepper pastes, and they are critical to the dish.

- 3 eggs
- 6 medium-sized white potatoes
- 2 chicken breasts
- Salt
- 1 (12-ounce) can evaporated milk, divided
- 6 slices of bread, crusts removed
- 3 tablespoons vegetable oil
- 1 medium red onion, diced, reserving some thin slices for finished dish
- 1 tablespoon minced garlic
- 1 (8-ounce) jar (about ¾ cup) of *ají amarillo* (see Note)
- 1 tablespoon *ají panca* (see Note)
- 1 cup chicken broth, divided
- Freshly ground pepper
- 1 tablespoon pecans, ground or finely chopped, reserving some for the finished dish, optional
- ¼ cup grated Parmesan cheese, reserving some for the finished dish, optional
- Olives, optional

TO MAKE HARD-COOKED EGGS: Place the eggs in a small pan, cover with water, and bring to a boil over medium-high heat. Remove the pan from the heat, cover the pan, and let sit for 15 minutes. Drain the water and add cold water, repeating until the eggs have cooled. Refrigerate until ready to use.

TO PREPARE THE POTATOES: Place the potatoes in a pot and cover with several inches of water. Bring the water to a boil over high heat and cook until the potatoes are tender when pierced with a fork, about 30 minutes. The potatoes can be peeled or unpeeled, but should remain whole.

TO MAKE THE CHICKEN: Place the chicken in a saucepan and cover with water. Add a bit of salt. Over high heat, bring the water to a boil, then reduce the heat to low and simmer gently until the chicken is tender and cooked through, about 20 minutes. Remove the chicken, reserving the broth. Cut the chicken into small pieces, or shred, and set aside.

Set aside ¼ cup of the evaporated milk. Place the bread in a shallow dish. Pour the remaining evaporated milk over the bread and leave it to soak.

In a large pot over low heat, warm 3 tablespoons vegetable oil. Add the onion and cook for 5 minutes. Add the garlic and cook for 2 minutes. Add the *ají amarillo* paste and the *ají panca* paste and cook until the oil separates from the sauce, about 10 to 12 minutes. This is a visual marker—cooking with your senses! Add the bread and stir with a wooden spoon (everything tastes better with a wooden spoon, says Jesus). Let it cook for about 10 more minutes.

Ají de Pollo

Add the chicken and ½ cup of the reserved chicken broth and cook for a few more minutes. Add more chicken broth, if needed, to make the sauce, which should not be watery like a soup broth, or too thick. It should be medium in viscosity. Add a splash of the remaining evaporated milk, along with salt, pepper, pecans (optional) and Parmesan (optional). Stir for 1 to 2 minutes.

TO SERVE: Peel the hard-cooked eggs and cut each in half. Cut each potato in half and place each one, cut side up, on a plate. Cover the potatoes with the *Ají de Pollo*. Add the egg halves and olives (optional) and scatter Parmesan (optional) and reserved onion and pecans (optional).

GUS AND KATE ROMERO

MEXICO AND POLAND

Perhaps their future was destined, given that Gustavo (Gus) Romero and Kate Kiernoziak met in a kitchen. He was chef at Credo in San Francisco, and she was sous-chef. Working long hours cemented their partnership and led to once-in-a-lifetime opportunities. They cooked for an event where First Lady Michelle Obama spoke, and—even better—they talked with her later. Knowing she liked tamales, they made a batch and sent those home with her. They like to think she tasted at least one. On another occasion, they cooked for an event for President Obama.

The pair moved to different cities to work at restaurants, from Miami and Chicago to Minneapolis, which was where they cooked food for the wedding of Kate's sister. After the occasion, Kate and Gus sat outside the hotel and sipped champagne when it hit them: they wanted to make a home in Minnesota.

When the pandemic hit in 2020, the restaurant where Gus worked shut down and Kate was pregnant. The one certainty that sustained them was that they knew they could cook. They

Gus and Kate Romero

began making meals once a week and selling them to family and friends. For the first few months, Kate and her sister made all the deliveries, often with her sister's young children in tow. They also made tortillas using heirloom corn and traditional nixtamalization techniques, which produces a healthier, sturdier, more flavorful tortilla. By midsummer, they opened Nixta in northeast Minneapolis. It is an artisanal *tortillería* with the tagline "Eat better tortillas." Three years later, next door to Nixta, they opened Oro by Nixta, with a full-service dining room. *Oro* means "gold" in Spanish, and this development felt golden. Oro was a 2024 semifinalist for the James Beard Foundation's Best New Restaurant Award.

Gus and Kate see themselves as pioneers in the tortilla revolution. "When you think about how many tortillas we consume," says Gus, "we should be consuming something good." They hope more people will make and eat these tortillas, so farmers might start growing the corn in Minnesota. In the meantime, they buy heritage corn from Mexico.

Gus Romero began his life in Tulancingo, in the state of Hidalgo, Mexico, where the seeds for his heirloom corn evangelism were planted. Due to his family's financial hardship, at age thirteen he set out for the United States. He met his mentor, Mario Maggi, in Florida, who encouraged him to train at a culinary school and who later sent him to Italy. Mario gave Gus his first official sous-chef position and showed him how to work with people. Mario also hired Kate at Credo, just before he sent Gus there. "The meddling mentor," they now call him.

Gus shares his mother's *mole verde* here. "It's something that is very close to me," he says. "It's one of those recipes that, when I make it, I have those memories of the smells that remind me of home." He got on the phone with his mother to make sure he wrote it down correctly, as he wanted to size the recipe for the home cook. She makes this *mole* like a version of salsa, with the addition of pepitas (raw pumpkin seeds), with the *mole* poured over chicken and rice. That was his birthday meal. When Gus is back in Mexico, she makes it for him. "I love *moles*," he says. "My last meal will have to be *mole* and a tortilla. I don't even need the meat."

Kate Kiernoziak was born in the south side of Chicago, where her parents had met, after growing up near each other in Poland, though they did not know it at the time. When Kate was two, her family moved to Poland, "the land of meat and potatoes, but no corn," she says. Kate describes the food of the Polish people as very simple, based on family farms that have cows and lambs, and fields where they grow beets, potatoes, and cabbage.

The family moved back to the United States when she was eleven years old and Kate started school without knowing English. "It was the worst first day of school ever," she remembers. It took years of English as a Second Language classes to get up to speed.

Her mother's love language is to cook for her family. When they returned to the United States, her mother made sure to maintain farm-fresh food, with meat from a butcher shop and vegetables from the farmers market in the summer. "Because my mom is always cooking, it was always so important for her to feed us good food and try new things," Kate says. She and her sister do the same today. "We all got the foodie gene from her."

Kate shares her recipe for cabbage rolls. "It's a meal all in itself," she says. "Like meatballs wrapped in cabbage, or like a Polish burrito." Once in San Francisco, when Kate was really missing home, she found a Polish deli and made cabbage rolls for a family meal at Credo. "That's when I started wanting to cook more Polish food."

Mole Verde con Pollo

Mole Verde con Pollo (Green Sauce with Chicken)

Makes 5 to 6 cups *mole verde*. Serves 8 with the chicken.

pepitas

CALDO DE POLLO (CHICKEN STOCK)

1 whole chicken, cut into 8 pieces, or 3 to 4 pounds chicken pieces of your choice (enough to feed your guests)

1 medium onion, cut in half

6 garlic cloves, peeled and left whole

2 bay leaves

1 large carrot, scrubbed and cut in large pieces

2 sprigs fresh thyme

MOLE VERDE

2 tablespoons oil

1 onion, diced

4 garlic cloves, chopped

5 jalapeño or serrano chiles, stemmed, seeded and chopped

1 cup toasted pepitas

1 tablespoon salt

½ teaspoon freshly ground black pepper

¼ teaspoon cumin seed

¼ teaspoon coriander seed

2 pounds tomatillos (about 20), husked and rinsed

2½ cups of the *Caldo de Pollo* broth

1 bunch fresh cilantro

1 bunch fresh epazote, leaves only

TO MAKE THE *CALDO*: Place the chicken, onion halves, garlic cloves, bay leaves, carrot, and thyme and 3 quarts (12 cups) water in a pot over high heat. Bring to a boil, then reduce heat to low and simmer, uncovered, until the chicken is fully cooked and reaches 165°F, about 20 to 25 minutes. Remove the chicken from the pot, set aside, and cover to keep warm. Set the remaining *caldo* in the pot aside.

TO MAKE THE *MOLE VERDE*: In a medium skillet over medium-high heat, warm up the oil. Add the diced onion, chopped garlic, and chiles, and cook until the onion is translucent, about 5 to 7 minutes. Add the pepitas, salt, black pepper, cumin seed, coriander seed, and tomatillos, and 2½ cups of the reserved *caldo*. Cook until the vegetables are soft and the pepitas are softening, about 25 minutes.

Working in small batches because the mixture is hot, carefully place the cooked vegetables, cilantro, and epazote leaves in a blender and process until smooth, with a gravy consistency. Add more *caldo* if the mixture is too thick.

TO SERVE: Pour the *mole verde* over the chicken or in a pool under it and serve with rice and tortillas. If preferred, bake the cooked chicken first at 375°F until the skin browns a bit, then place the chicken on a plate with the *mole verde*.

NOTE: Pepitas are raw pumpkin seeds. Find them in the bulk section at the supermarket or food co-op. They are available either raw or toasted/roasted. If raw, toast them in a dry skillet over low heat until they become fragrant. Epazote leaves can be found at Mexican markets.

Cabbage Rolls

Makes about 18 to 20

NOTE: Plan ahead to cook the rice and the barley. To remove the stalk from the cabbage, you will need a sharp knife. If yours is dull, you could instead carefully remove the cabbage leaves when the head is intact, then drop the leaves individually in the boiling water for 30 seconds to blanch them. This recipe uses both a 9- by 13-inch pan and an 8-inch square pan.

CABBAGE ROLLS

1 cup cooked rice
1 cup cooked pearled barley
1 large green cabbage or 2 small ones
½ pound bacon, chopped
1 cup chopped yellow onion
1 pound lean ground beef
½ pound ground pork
1 tablespoon salt

SAUCE

1 (14- to 15-ounce) can tomato sauce
1 cup chicken stock
1 teaspoon salt
½ teaspoon freshly ground black pepper
1 cup heavy cream

TO MAKE THE CABBAGE ROLLS: Prepare the rice and barley according to package directions. Remove the stalk from the bottom of the cabbage head with a sharp knife. Place the whole cabbage in a large pot filled with water. Cover and place over high heat. Bring to a boil and then reduce the heat to medium. Cook until the cabbage leaves become bright green and pliable, about 3 to 5 minutes. Make sure to not overcook so the leaves maintain their shape. Carefully remove the head of cabbage and place on a cutting board until it cools down.

Cook the bacon in a sauté pan over medium heat. After the bacon is done, take it out and leave the fat in the pan. Cook the onions in the bacon fat until translucent. In a large bowl combine the ground beef, pork, onion, bacon, barley, rice, and 1 tablespoon salt. Place in the refrigerator until ready to use.

TO MAKE THE SAUCE: In a medium pot over medium heat, combine the tomato sauce, chicken stock, 1 teaspoon salt, and pepper. Bring to a boil and remove the pot from the heat. Add the heavy cream and set aside.

Preheat the oven to 350°F. Once the cabbage has cooled, peel the leaves off the head one by one, being careful not to rip them. Use a small knife to trim and remove the stalk at the bottom of the leaf.

TO MAKE THE ROLLS: Spread about ¾ cup of the sauce across the bottom of a 9- by 13-inch baking pan. Use about ½ cup sauce for the 8-inch square pan. Put 2 to 3 (or more) generous tablespoons of filling on the bottom half of a cabbage leaf. Fold up the bottom, fold in the sides, and roll forward until the cabbage leaf covers the filling. Place the stuffed cabbage leaves into the prepared pans in neat rows and pour the rest of the sauce over and between the cabbage rolls in the two pans. (The large pan will hold about 12 rolls; the smaller one about 6 to 8.) Cover the pans with aluminum foil and bake until heated through, about 50 to 60 minutes. Serve hot.

Cabbage Rolls

EMILIA OLABISI FATMATA SMITH

SIERRA LEONE

Emilia Olabisi Fatmata Smith

Emilia Olabisi Fatmata Smith grew up in Sierra Leone, a country in West Africa on the coast of the Atlantic Ocean. She spent her early years in two small rural villages, and then moved with her father and stepmother to Freetown, the capital of Sierra Leone, when she was about six years old. Her early life was disrupted when her father went to the United States in 1989 for medical care, joining her uncle who already was in Minnesota. Shortly after that, war broke out in Sierra Leone, when a rebel army attempted a coup. When the war in neighboring Liberia overtook Sierra Leone, the brutality left many seeking refuge in neighboring countries and the world at large.

Given the war, Emilia's father, a former police-force communications officer in his homeland, could not return home. He stayed in the United States and filed for political asylum. Senator Paul Wellstone, a long-standing supporter of peace and human rights, signed his papers. "The African community in Minnesota wept like he was one of us when he died," says Emilia about the senator.

Emilia stayed in Sierra Leone with her stepmother, brother, and sister. Her stepmother, a teacher and seamstress, served as a mentor to many and helped those who struggled, whether it was troubled teens, people in difficult marriages, or those facing hard times. Her efforts would influence Emilia in later years.

About eight years after her father left, Emilia and her family were reunited with him in the United States, with the help of a local church. Coming from tropical Sierra Leone, Emilia vividly recalls the cold March weather in Minnesota, where they were met with jackets, mittens, and hats. "Our first morning, we were just in awe," she says. "Everything was new. We each came with two pieces of luggage and a carry-on. Our whole life was in those bags." But they also were in culture shock. "By that time, my dad was too American for us, and we were too African for him."

The reunion was not easy. "Life was bumpy for us," Emilia says. "We were learning America." In Sierra Leone, they did not have 24-hour electricity, house payments, or credit cards. The learning curve was steep. In addition to a new culture, they continued to care for family members in Sierra Leone. "When you're in America, everybody back home is calling, and you have to help," she says. "Your paycheck is not even enough to take care of yourself, but you have to take care of other people."

Emilia's father made sure they all arrived with transcripts and medical records, documents that they carried with them. The process was unexpectedly efficient, with immigration/residency papers processed a few months after their arrival, and school for Emilia at the University of Minnesota that fall.

"My dad made sure we went to school right away," she says. "For our family, we saw education as the way out." Her brother went on to get a master's degree in engineering and her sister earned a PhD in audiology. Emilia graduated from the university and went into banking, where she has had a career at several major financial institutions. Like her stepmother, she is a natural mentor. Having experienced firsthand the challenges of resettlement, she understands the critical need for advisors.

"Who you associate with can make or break you," she says. "Without mentors, kids turn to gangs because this is where they are accepted." Emilia works with the Sierra Leonean community, supporting people of all ages through her work with OneVillage Partners, and the Sierra Leone Community in Minnesota, and as a founder and mentor for Pan African Girls Engagement Initiative.

What is the same in both Sierra Leone and the United States is what happens in the kitchen. They always cooked in large amounts for their extended families. "No matter how poor you are, there's always some way you can help," Emilia says. By age nine, she was cooking. By age twelve, she was walking to the market for food and preparing a meal for the whole family—and more. "We don't RSVP," says Emilia of fellow Sierra Leoneans. "You hear of an event and you just show up, because everyone is invited." In fact, the meal means more than what's on the table. "Food always equals love in Sierra Leone," she says.

Emilia offers a favorite here, the recipe for coconut cakes, which would be called cookies in the United States. This recipe makes use of coconut flakes, though in Sierra Leone she would have used fresh coconut. *Bi-ka. Bi-ka/Tenki!* Thank you!

Coconut Cakes

Coconut Cakes

Makes 10 to 12 cakes (cookies)

- 1 cup unsweetened coconut flakes
- ½ cup granulated sugar
- 1 tablespoon plus 2 teaspoons peeled and finely grated fresh ginger

NOTE: In Sierra Leone, these would be made with fresh coconut. For this recipe, packaged coconut flakes are more accessible.

Put the coconut flakes in a saucepan over medium-high heat and add just enough water to cover (about ½ cup). Add the sugar and stir until dissolved. Add the grated ginger and boil until the sugar changes color and caramelizes.

Cover your work surface with waxed paper. Place tablespoon-sized scoops of the coconut mixture on the paper. Allow to cool thoroughly and store in an airtight container.

coconut flakes

KITCHENS OF RESILIENCE

Resilience reflects grit and determination, as well as the courage to move forward. Conchy Morgan showed these qualities when her mother sent her and her sister, as children, from Cuba to the United States to keep them safe. The war zone of Democratic Republic of Congo inspired Ingrid Kubisa and her family to take up humanitarian work. Hiba Al-Hasnawi, a mechanical engineer in Iraq, fled her country after attempts on her life. In the United States, she has taught English as a Second Language classes. As a child, Maiyia Vang survived a harrowing trek from Laos to reach safety and freedom, and now helps others who seek to build new lives in Minnesota. Blaise Masinga left the political turmoil of Democratic Republic of Congo for South Africa, looking for refuge, education, and a career. Eventually, fearing for his safety there, he headed to the United States to rebuild his life. Ghulam Jamili and his family faced danger in Afghanistan, where his sons were targeted by the Taliban for their work with the U.S. government. All found comfort and strength around a crowded dinner table, filled with food from their homelands.

CONCEPCIÓN DE LA CARIDAD DIAZ MORGAN

CUBA

In the aftermath of Fidel Castro's rise to power in Cuba in 1959, Cuban parents faced life-changing decisions to ensure the well-being of their children. Many chose to send their children, unaccompanied, to the United States until they could join them, or the children could safely return to Cuba. Concepción (Conchy) de la Caridad Diaz Morgan was one of those children.

Between 1960 and 1962, more than 14,000 unaccompanied minors ages 6 to 18 were sent to the United States through Operation Pedro Pan ("Peter Pan"), a covert program that included the U.S. State Department, the Catholic Church (in both Cuba and the United States), private schools, and families. Once in the United States, the children were sent to live in various locations across the country. Some had relatives in the United States they could live with, but many did not. Those without relatives were placed in Catholic boarding facilities or other accommodations, with the expectation that the families would later be reunited.

Concepción (Conchy) de la Caridad Diaz Morgan

Conchy was born in Matanzas, Cuba, a cultural center near Havana. By 1959, her mother was a widow with four children. When Fidel Castro shut down the Catholic schools in Cuba and communist indoctrination increased, Conchy's mother, concerned about the future, took a leap of faith. In the spring of 1962, she sent fifteen-year-old Conchy and her twelve-year-old sister to the United States. The older children stayed in Cuba with their mother.

Conchy never anticipated her stay would be permanent. She expected to return when Cuba stabilized, perhaps after one year at most, but that never happened. In the fall of 1962, commercial flights between Cuba and the United States ceased due to the Cuban Missile Crisis. Conchy would not see her mother again for two decades, or her two older siblings for twenty-eight years.

When she and her sister arrived in Miami, they were initially placed in a Pedro Pan camp in Florida City, where they awaited placement. Eventually they were relocated to David City, Nebraska, a quiet town of 2,300 people, a stark contrast to her home in Matanzas, a bustling city of 80,000. There Conchy lived at Casa del Cristo Rey, a group home for Pedro Pan high-school girls that Franciscan nuns had established. She expected that her sister would accompany her but, after learning that her sister was to be sent to an orphanage in Omaha because she was too young for Cristo Rey, Conchy protested. As a result, a foster family was found in David City for her sister. Conchy and her sister lived near each other for the next year. Then many of the Cuban families were reunited and Cristo Rey closed. Conchy moved in with her sister's foster family, spending her remaining two high-school years there. Her sister continued to live with the foster family for three more years.

Conchy's mother had encouraged her to continue her studies, so following high school, Conchy listened to her mother's advice and attended the University of Nebraska in Lincoln. At university, Conchy lived with a Cuban family who had recently emigrated to the United States. They provided room and board while Conchy studied and worked at a hospital as a nurse's aide. She graduated from the university, married a Nebraskan, and moved to Ann Arbor, Michigan, where he was attending law school. Following his graduation, they moved to New York City, where her husband was stationed in the Navy. In those years, Conchy taught high school in suburban Detroit and then Manhattan before eventually moving to Minnesota with her husband.

Reflecting on her move to the United States, Conchy says, "I can't pinpoint when or how, but as more parents joined their children, I knew it wasn't going to happen for us. We were never going back. It was very hard." Conchy wrote home regularly and tried to stay upbeat and not reflect that she and her sister were homesick or that anything was amiss. When she first tried to return to her homeland for a visit, the Cuban government refused her request. Conchy finally saw her mother again for the first time in 1982 when she traveled to the United States, by which time Conchy was married and had a son. Her family reunited in stages over the years.

Conchy has returned to Cuba on three occasions in more recent years, which were emotional trips for her. Her husband and children have joined her, came to know her brother in Cuba, and visited the family home. Conchy travels regularly to Miami to reconnect with other family members and when she does, they always eat Cuban food, especially the Cuban "comfort food" *picadillo*. Both of her children love *picadillo* and make it at home. When visiting her son on Mother's Day, he is certain to make it for her.

Picadillo

Serves 10

- 6 very ripe tomatoes
- 2 pounds ground beef, preferably sirloin
- 2 medium onions, finely chopped
- 2 garlic cloves, minced
- 1 large green bell pepper, seeded and cored, and finely chopped
- 1 tablespoon olive oil
- Salt and freshly ground black pepper, to taste
- 1 tablespoon brown sugar
- 2 tablespoons red wine vinegar
- ¼ cup small pimento-stuffed green olives
- ½ cup raisins
- 1 tablespoon capers
- ½ cup red wine
- Fresh flat-leaf parsley, chopped, for garnish
- Cooked white rice
- Cooked black beans

TO PEEL TOMATOES: Drop them in boiling water for 30 to 60 seconds and remove. Set aside until cool enough to handle, then rub the skins off. Dice the tomatoes.

TO MAKE *PICADILLO*: In a large skillet over medium heat, brown the meat with ¼ cup water, stirring to break up any large chunks. Drain and transfer the meat to a bowl. Place the onions, garlic, bell pepper, and olive oil in the same large skillet and sauté over medium-high heat, stirring until the onions are golden brown.

Return the meat to the pan, then stir in the tomatoes, salt and pepper, brown sugar, vinegar, olives, raisins, capers, and red wine. Reduce the heat to low and cook until the meat is tender and the sauce is thick, about 50 to 60 minutes. Garnish with parsley and serve on a bed of white rice with black beans.

Picadillo

INGRID KUBISA
DEMOCRATIC REPUBLIC OF CONGO

Ingrid Kubisa

Ingrid Kubisa has lived with war much of her life. Born in Bukavu in Democratic Republic of Congo (DRC) in 1996, peace was an elusive concept. "You can hear about the reconciliation from the outside, but when you live it, you don't see this," she says. Ingrid recalls that, as a grade-schooler, she received a warning one day not to go to school. She stayed home and later that day war broke out, with gunfire and bombs continuing for several weeks.

Ingrid became involved in humanitarian work early. In 2001, she traveled the countryside with family members as they searched for children as young as seven years old who had been recruited to be soldiers during the civil war in the DRC. She recalls playing with children traumatized by the war. "Our family sings," she says, "and we would go sing for victims of war." Ingrid's family received asylum protection in the United States in 2016.

The journey from the DRC to the United States was difficult. Ingrid's mother received a call one night instructing the family to go to Burundi for interviews for U.S. visas. They could not share this plan or say goodbye to anyone. Getting to Burundi was a challenge. Ingrid and one of her sisters were away at college, so they took one car for the four-hour drive. Her mother and other four siblings used a second car and traveled on little-used roads on a journey that took thirteen hours. Ingrid and her sister waited for hours in Burundi, not knowing if the others would arrive. Fortunately they did, and the family received visas and fled to the United States.

The transition to the United States was difficult, particularly for Ingrid's mother, because the cultural conventions were so different. For example, no one dropped by unexpectedly, as was the custom in her homeland. She could not envision having to schedule gatherings and invite guests to come and eat. "I grew up in a house that was offering food," Ingrid says. "Food is something you have to share to show love."

And the food was so different. It took time to meet people who could help them find African foods: plantains, cassava, special fish, rice and beans. There were no local restaurants making Congolese food, so Ingrid's mother started catering. Today, their family shares Congolese food wherever they can—at home, for events, for potlucks, and for this cookbook. Ingrid offers a recipe here for a traditional Congolese dish of marinated fish.

Ingrid recently married in her homeland and more than a year later waits for her husband to be permitted to join her in the United States. In the meantime, she continues to share a home with her parents and five siblings.

Ingrid and one sister graduated from Gustavus Adolphus College, where they were the college's first two graduates from the DRC. Ingrid works in human rights. Another sister completed her master's degree in global health education and teaches at St. Catherine University. The family shares a common vision: working in the United States to help those in the DRC. They all look for opportunities to return to their homeland, which could transpire if new leadership in the DRC allows dual citizenship. In the meantime, Ingrid is pursuing her personal goal: to be part of the people who make change. She plans to eventually open a youth-run coffee shop in the DRC.

She invites others to share a Congolese dinner at her home. No need to call first. Drop-ins are welcome.

Marinated Tilapia or Mackerel

Serves 6 or more, depending on the size of the fish

½ onion, roughly chopped in quarters

2 garlic cloves

½ green bell pepper, seeded, cored, and diced

Salt, to taste

1 teaspoon freshly ground black pepper

1 teaspoon ground ginger

Fish seasoning (such as Old Bay), to taste

All-purpose seasoning, such as Vegeta, or alternative (see Note)

2 Maggi cubes or 2 other bouillon cubes of your choice (see Note)

Freshly squeezed juice of 1 lime or lemon (about 2 tablespoons)

3 tilapia or mackerel fillets

In a blender or food processor, combine the onion, garlic, and green pepper with the salt, black pepper, ginger, fish seasoning, all-purpose seasoning, and Maggi cubes, along with the lime or lemon juice. Process until the mixture is a purée.

Place the fish in a low dish with sides and add the marinade, setting a little aside to brush on the fish later. (Do not reuse the marinade that has been on the raw fish.) Let the marinade sit for about 5 to 10 minutes if the fish is to be grilled, or 30 minutes if it will be fried.

Grill or fry (the latter in a little oil) over medium-high heat for 4 minutes per side, brushing the reserved marinade on each side, until the fish flakes easily with a fork.

NOTE: Maggi seasoning comes in liquid, cube, and powdered forms. It enhances food with a deep, umami-rich flavor. If grilling tilapia, using a fish basket is helpful as the fish is very delicate. Vegeta is an all-purpose seasoning with dehydrated vegetables, spices, and MSG.

Maggi seasoning

Marinated Tilapia or Mackerel

HIBA AL-HASNAWI

IRAQ

Hiba Al-Hasnawi was born in Baghdad, Iraq, and grew up during the Iraq War (2003–11). As the conflict began to wind down in 2009, Hiba joined efforts to redefine U.S.–Iraqi relations through participation in the Iraqi and American Reconciliation Project (IARP), an organization that worked to build relationships and reconciliation between the sister cities of Minneapolis and Najaf, Iraq.

Hiba came to Minneapolis with an Iraqi delegation from IARP on three occasions for the purposes of training, cultural exchange, and support for Iraqi children. Despite these noteworthy goals, prominent militia in Iraq were suspicious of individuals and organizations associated with the United States. After multiple attempts on her life, Hiba fled to the United States in 2017, leaving her former life behind, including her two children.

Recalling prior trips to Minnesota and acquaintances there, Hiba came directly to Minneapolis, and spent the next six months looking for organizations that could help her with asylum. Only a week before her visa was to expire, the Advocates for Human Rights answered her call. A volunteer spoke to her in Arabic, reassured her, and introduced her to an immigration lawyer who helped her apply for asylum. Five years later, she received her green card. Her lawyer also assisted in seeking visas for Hiba's children who stayed in Iraq when she left. Both of Hiba's now-adult children have arrived in the United States, where they have been able to build a new life together.

Though Hiba attended college in Baghdad and trained as a mechanical engineer, she cannot practice her profession in the United States because she is unable to obtain her transcripts and credentials from Iraq. Since arriving in the United States, she has taught English as a Second Language and worked for several years at Literacy Minnesota Open Door Learning Center, where she pursued her passion for education and connecting people with resources. She continues to look forward as she plans for training in social work, where she will continue to focus on helping those in need. Her motto: "Tomorrow is another day."

Hiba smiles when she talks of foods from home: *baba ghanoush* (roasted eggplant dip), *biryani* (a rice dish with meat, vegetables and spices), and hummus (mashed chickpea dip). You can smell the spices—cardamom, cumin, and cinnamon—as she describes the dishes. Hiba loves to learn about new cultures, meet new people, and make new friends. Sharing food is part of that. When Hiba is invited to a friend's holiday celebration, she will eat their foods and bring her own dishes to share. "These dishes are part of me," she says.

Hiba Al-Hasnawi

Baba Ghanoush

Baba Ghanoush (Smoked Eggplant Dip)

Makes about 2 cups

- 4 medium eggplants
- Salt, to taste
- 1 garlic clove, peeled and grated
- Freshly squeezed juice of ½ lemon, more if needed
- 1 tablespoon olive oil, plus more for serving if desired
- Freshly ground black pepper, to taste
- 3 tablespoons tahini
- 3 tablespoons plain yogurt
- Kalamata olives and fresh mint for decoration, optional
- Pita bread, crackers, or fresh vegetables, for serving

Poke the eggplants with a fork and grill whole over medium-high heat, about 15 minutes on each side. When they are done, they should look black and blistered all over, with smoke coming out of the poked holes. Though the grill gives a nice smoked flavor, if one is unavailable, the eggplants can be roasted in the oven. Cut the eggplants in half and place them flesh-side down on a greased baking sheet. Roast at 425°F until they are blistered and soft, about 40 minutes.

Remove the eggplants from the grill or oven and set aside to cool. When ready, cut open the eggplants, remove the seeds and skin and discard both, saving the interior flesh. In a medium bowl, mash the eggplant flesh with a fork, removing any remaining blistered or black skin.

Salt the eggplant mash to taste. Add the grated garlic, lemon juice, olive oil, black pepper, tahini, and yogurt, and mix together. Taste and add more lemon juice, if preferred. Stir the mixture until smooth. If desired, serve with a drizzle of olive oil or top the *baba ghanoush* with olives and fresh mint. Serve with pita bread, crackers, or fresh vegetables.

Iraqi Chicken *Biryani*

Serves 8 to 10

NOTE: This dish includes chicken, potatoes, onions, rice, and vermicelli. You will be using the same spices for many steps.

CHICKEN

- 3½ pounds chicken, with or without skin (either thighs or breast)
- 3 to 4 cardamom pods
- 1 cinnamon stick
- 5 to 6 whole cloves
- 1½ teaspoons salt
- ½ teaspoon ground turmeric
- Small onion, cut in half
- 1 cup slivered almonds, for serving

RICE

- 2 cups basmati rice
- 3 cups reserved chicken broth, or water
- 3 to 4 cardamom pods
- 1 cinnamon stick
- 5 to 6 whole cloves

TO PREPARE THE CHICKEN: Place the chicken in a large pot with 3 to 4 cardamom pods, 1 cinnamon stick, 5 to 6 whole cloves, 1½ teaspoons salt, ½ teaspoon turmeric, and the onion halves. Add water to cover, about 8 cups. Bring to a boil over high heat and keep boiling, covered, for 5 minutes. Reduce the heat and simmer gently for 20 minutes. Remove the chicken from the pot, strain the liquid and set aside.

Place the chicken on a baking sheet and broil it at 500°F on the top oven rack for 2 to 3 minutes to brown a bit. Do not broil longer, or the meat will become tough. If using chicken breasts, cut each into two or three large pieces. Set the meat aside.

TO TOAST THE ALMONDS: Preheat the oven to 350°F. Arrange the almonds in a single layer on a baking sheet and toast them in the oven for about 5 to 8 minutes. Remove the baking sheet from the oven, transfer the almonds to a plate, and cool completely.

TO PREPARE THE RICE: Rinse the rice in cold water until it runs clear; drain. Place the rice in a pot with 3 cups of either water or the reserved chicken broth, and add 3 to 4 fresh cardamom pods, 1 cinnamon stick, and 5 to 6 whole cloves. Bring to a boil over high heat, then reduce the heat and simmer, covered, for about 20 minutes. Or use a rice cooker if you prefer.

POTATOES, VERMICELLI, AND VEGETABLES

- 3 large potatoes, peeled, or 24 ounces little potatoes (1½ pounds total)
- 4 tablespoons oil, divided
- ½ teaspoon ground turmeric
- ½ teaspoon ground cumin
- ½ teaspoon salt
- 1 teaspoon yellow curry powder, divided
- 1 onion, thinly sliced
- 2 teaspoons freshly ground black pepper, divided
- 1 (12-ounce) bag frozen peas and carrots
- 1 (17.6 ounce) package vermicelli (Hiba uses the Ziyad brand)
- ¾ cup golden raisins
- 1 teaspoon ground cardamom
- 1 pinch saffron, dissolved in 2 tablespoons water

vermicelli

TO PREPARE THE POTATO, VERMICELLI, AND VEGETABLE MIXTURE: Scrub the potatoes and cut into ½-inch cubes. Place the potatoes in a 12-inch or larger skillet with 2 tablespoons oil. Cover and cook over medium-low heat, stirring occasionally, for about 10 minutes. Add ½ teaspoon turmeric, ½ teaspoon cumin, ½ teaspoon salt, and ½ teaspoon yellow curry powder, and cook until the potatoes are tender and golden, stirring frequently. Transfer the potatoes to a plate or baking sheet lined with paper towels to absorb any extra oil.

Add the sliced onions to the same large pan with 1 tablespoon oil, 1 teaspoon black pepper, and ½ teaspoon yellow curry powder. Increase the heat to medium, stirring occasionally, and cook until tender. Remove from the heat and place on paper towels to drain the oil.

Add the peas and carrots to the same large skillet (if still frozen, add 2 tablespoons water) and cook over medium heat, stirring occasionally, until cooked through. Remove the peas and carrots from the skillet, place in a large bowl or pan, and add the drained potatoes and onions.

Add the vermicelli to the same large skillet and toss with about 1 tablespoon oil. Cook over medium heat, stirring occasionally, until the noodles begin to brown, about 5 to 10 minutes. Add 2½ cups hot water and a pinch of salt, then cover and simmer, stirring occasionally, until the noodles are tender but firm, about 10 minutes.

Add the vermicelli to the cooked potatoes, carrots and peas, and onions, and toss with raisins, 1 teaspoon ground cardamom, and 1 teaspoon black pepper.

TO ASSEMBLE THE *BIRYANI*: Spread the rice on a large platter and drizzle with the saffron water. Top with the potato, vermicelli, and vegetable mix, then arrange chicken pieces on top. To finish, sprinkle with the toasted almonds.

MAIYIA VANG

HMONG

Maiyia Vang

The Hmong are survivors. "It is ingrained in our blood," says Maiyia Vang. She and her family survived the month-long trek from Laos to a Thai refugee camp, one treacherous step at a time.

The Hmong people have no formal country to call their own. Historically, they were nomads who lived throughout China and Southeast Asia, primarily in Laos, Thailand, and Vietnam. As the Vietnam War came to a close in 1975, the Hmong were targeted for assisting the United States during the war. Many chose to leave their countries in search of safety and freedom.

Maiyia's family escaped when she was four years old. Her father led the migration of their entire village of more than thirty families, coordinating the journey in secret and providing a short list of items for the villagers to prepare for the expedition. The villagers lived life normally during the day and secretly put away provisions at night, hiding packets of rice and other supplies outside the village. Once they set out for Thailand, they hid during the daytime and traveled by night. Each one followed the shadow ahead, staying on the path carved out by the scouts, walking in the steps of the person in front of them to avoid triggering hidden landmines.

In addition to their rice, they ate whatever they could find along the way: roots dug from the ground, wild vegetables along the paths, fish from the rivers. Maiyia's two younger sisters were carried by her parents. She and her uncle, who was her age, walked through the jungle, sometimes barefoot, at other times with plastic sandals.

She remembers the fear throughout their long journey, which took more than thirty days, during which many villagers died along the way. The group finally reached the Mekong River, with safety waiting on the other side. However, many people were lost to its currents trying to reach the other side. Under the guidance of her father, Maiyia's family made it across the river on plastic inner tubes tied together, pushing against the tide in the dark of night and arriving in the morning. Her family found their way to a refugee camp. Less than a year later, they were flown to the United States, landing in Lansing, Michigan, wearing sandals in the snow.

The family gravitated to Minnesota, where their immediate relatives and other Hmong refugees had settled, prompted by sponsorship and resettlement assistance from organizations such as the Lutheran church. Minnesota was more prepared for and welcoming to new immigrants, in part because of the churches, and also because of such organizations as the Advocates for Human Rights. Maiyia has joined this work through her role as the operations manager of the immigration law group at Fredrikson & Byron law firm, assisting others who seek to build new lives here.

The Hmong people are made up of eighteen clans, and the Vang and Yang clans are the largest. "All Hmong people are related," Maiyia says. "If we sit down and talk, we see the connections." She was born in the mountains of Laos, where her family had little access to many seasonings. Meat was a luxury and rarely served. Over decades, as the Hmong adapted to new lands, they ate whatever they could find. The Hmong diet is highly plant-based, centered on grains, vegetables, and fish. The food doesn't require many ingredients to provide a simple, clean taste.

Maiyia's recipe is for a chicken soup made with lemongrass and many herbs that offer medicinal benefits, as well as a distinct Hmong flavor. This soup plays a humble but important role as it is served daily for a month to Hmong women after they have given birth. The Hmong tradition strictly limits what women are to eat during this time: soup broth with herbs and chicken, as well as rice. Several hospitals in Minnesota where many Hmong women give birth now prepare this for their patients. Maiyia ate this after each of her five children were born. The Hmong herbs, which are gathered in a large bunch of eight to ten different types, include many that do not have English names. They are seasonal in the fall and summer, and usually available at Hmong markets and some farmers markets. Ask for the "chicken soup" herbs and the vendors will know what you're looking for.

THAI

The tapestry tells the history of the Hmong people.

Hmong Chicken Soup

Hmong Chicken Soup

Makes 6 or more servings

This soup is served primarily for postpartum diets or as health recovery soup in the Hmong culture. Maiyia has used these herbs based on what her mother and grandmother told her, and they helped her recover over thirty days of postpartum.

- 1 full-size lemongrass stalk
- 1 small fresh ginger root, peeled and sliced
- 1 medium-sized organic chicken (or 2 small Cornish hens), cleaned well and cut into smaller pieces with the bones
- 1 teaspoon salt, or 1 teaspoon mushroom seasoning, or 1 cube chicken bouillon, or 1 teaspoon fish sauce
- Freshly ground black pepper, to taste
- 1 package Hmong chicken soup herbs, washed well (see Note)
- Hot cooked white rice

Put 12 to 14 cups water in a medium pot over high heat and add the lemongrass and ginger root. Bring to a boil and add the chicken pieces. Add the salt (or mushroom seasoning or bouillon cube or fish sauce) and black pepper to the water. Cook at a brisk boil for 15 to 20 minutes (depending on the size of the poultry).

Add the Hmong herbs, stir, and bring to boil again, about 5 minutes. Remove from the heat and remove the lemongrass. Let the broth cool slightly before serving with a side of white rice.

NOTE: There is no substitute for the Hmong chicken soup herbs, which are available in Hmong markets and some farmers markets.

Hmong chicken soup herbs

BLAISE MASINGA
DEMOCRATIC REPUBLIC OF CONGO

Blaise Masinga

Blaise Masinga was born in the western part of Democratic Republic of Congo (DRC). Beginning in the 1990s, struggle was a part of everyday life in that country, but early lessons for him in income disparities, injustice, and human rights fueled a life of activism and a passion to make a difference. Blaise was raised in a Mennonite home where faith and ethics were central to their lives. His mother was his mentor in life. "She was an advocate in the community and had a big heart," he says.

Blaise graduated from the Catholic School of Fraternity in Kikwit, after which he wanted to further his education. Political turmoil, however, had closed the university. At age eighteen, he left his family and community and fled the DRC, becoming a refugee in South Africa. All alone, he quickly learned that South Africa was not the refuge he needed. Initially, he was not welcome in South Africa's apartheid system. He was the wrong color and refugees faced barriers everywhere: in naturalization, employment, education, and respect. "The hatred of refugees was unbelievable," Blaise says. But he persevered and began to build a life. He attended university, married, and started a family.

His business career began to flourish. He started his career as a consultant for Black Economic Empowerment, a South African government initiative with the goal of facilitating broader participation in the economy by people of color. In 2010, Blaise was named the business manager for Central Africa for Bayer Crop Science in South Africa. Despite this success, he could not ignore the rampant racism and discrimination. Fearing for his and his family's safety, he had no choice but to leave.

He moved his wife and children to the DRC before seeking haven in the United States for himself in 2012. There he found himself alone again, not knowing that it would be four years before he would see his family, who themselves suffered the trauma of being refugees. Stateless and struggling to find his way in a new country, Blaise connected with the Advocates for Human Rights and the Center for Victims of Torture, who assisted with basic resources and a referral to a pro-bono lawyer who helped him gain asylum. He became a U.S. citizen in 2021.

Blaise reunited with his family in the United States and rebuilt his life here. Needing additional professional credentials, he attended the University of St. Thomas for managerial training and earned a mini-master's degree in project management. He spent a decade working as a banker in financial institutions. His years as a refugee sharpened his focus and led him to return to where he began—wanting to make a difference in people's lives. He earned a degree in community development at Metropolitan State University and, in 2020, started the Masinga Foundation, dedicated to mentoring and supporting Congolese youth and communities. With an office in the DRC, the main project is a self-financed pharmacy that he hopes to transform into a full clinic to help more people in need.

"In everything I have done, I have tried to make a difference in people's lives," he says. "I come from a country where people need lots of help." Blaise and his family are firmly rooted in the United States, but given his work with the Masinga Foundation, the DRC is never far away.

While his children enjoy American food, Blaise and his wife continue to cook the traditional foods of his homeland, dishes that his mother prepared for him for almost twenty years and that he carried with him first to South Africa and then to the United States. For Blaise, these are the foods that define home, and he still eats them every day, with *fufu* and plantains among them.

Semolina *Fufu*

Serves 2 to 3

1 cup semolina flour

NOTE: *Fufu* is a dough-like food often made from mashed cassava that has been boiled, pounded, and rounded into balls. Semolina flour can be substituted for the mashed cassava, as it is here. An alternative: Pounded yam flour is available in African markets and is used for a different variation of *fufu*.

Bring 2 cups water to a boil in a large saucepan. Add the semolina flour slowly, stirring constantly with a spatula or wooden spoon until all the flour has been added and the water is incorporated into the semolina. Continue to stir briskly until the *fufu* is smooth and free of lumps.

Using a spatula, separate the dough from the pan and transfer to a plate or a bowl, shaping it into a large round circle or dividing it into individual round portions. Cover tightly with plastic wrap until ready to serve.

To eat, break off a small piece of *fufu*, about the size of two or three grapes, and knead together a few times between your thumb and forefingers. Dip the *fufu* into a sauce or wrap it around a bit of meat, fish, rice, or vegetable.

Semolina *Fufu*

Fried Plantains

Serves 2 to 4

2 or 3 plantains, green or ripe yellow
Canola oil for frying

NOTE: Green plantains are less sweet than yellow ones.

Peel the plantains and slice them into diagonal pieces.

Add enough oil to a pan to cover the bottom by ¼ inch. Warm the oil over medium heat, and add the plantain slices in a single layer. Fry, turning occasionally, until they are your preferred color. Remove and place on a paper towel to drain, and serve.

plantains

GHULAM JAMILI

AFGHANISTAN

In the Afghan culture, it would be disrespectful to call an elder by his first name, which is why he is referred to as Mr. Jamili here.

Ghulam Sarwar Jamili had to leave Afghanistan in 2021 for his safety. Many members of his family were at risk when U.S. forces left Afghanistan, and the Taliban returned to power. Its first targets were Afghans who had worked with the U.S. government or other affiliated organizations, and that included some of Mr. Jamili's sons. U.S. employers directed their at-risk workers to switch locations nightly while they developed evacuation plans.

One night, Mr. Jamili's oldest son received a call from his employer. He was directed to meet a bus late that night that would transport him and some family members to the nearest available airport in Mazar e Shareef. After a twelve-hour bus ride, they arrived at the airport and were flown to a military base in Doha, Qatar. Mr. Jamili and his wife were part of this group. After a month in

Ghulam Jamili

Qatar, they boarded another plane with little information about their destination. They thought they were headed to the United States, but instead landed at Camp Bondsteel, another military base, this time in the Republic of Kosovo. Months later, after obtaining U.S. visas, they were brought to Virginia to await passports. Their last stop was Minnesota, where they eventually connected with the Advocates for Human Rights. Four of Mr. Jamili's children and their families are now in the United States, and they have all resettled in Virginia.

Mr. Jamili does not speak English. With his son acting as translator, Mr. Jamili repeatedly expressed his gratitude to the many people who have helped his family rebuild their lives. He also shared what continues to haunt him: the separation from his friends and relatives. "That's a void that will always be there," he says. In Kabul, Mr. Jamili was a well-loved and revered friend and advisor. Neighbors stopped by daily to converse, and if they had a dispute with others, they would come to him for resolution. That status was hard-earned through years of activism protecting his community and advocating for education and empowerment for girls and women. Now in the United States he is starting over, having left his home, his land, and part of his family behind.

One connection to home is through food. In Afghanistan, Mr. Jamili's extended family—nine adult children, some with spouses and children—lived together in Kabul and spent summers in the remote village of Guldara (Valley of the Flowers), where they had large gardens and fruit trees. The family took care of one another, cooking and eating together.

As in other Afghan households, rice was a centerpiece for all meals. Other foods were positioned on it, cut in sizes that allowed the family to eat with their hands. The significance of rice at the Afghan table is such that, if someone wants to show respect, they offer rice. If a family is not able to offer rice, they will apologize, saying, "We love you so much, but we were not able to make rice."

With his recipe for *Uzbek Palaw*, Mr. Jamili offers rice in a traditional Afghan dish made of layers of a special long-grain rice (Golden Sella) that is served with chunks of beef, onion, and carrots. *Palaw* spices, which can be hand-ground or purchased in Indian groceries, provide the unique cardamom flavor. The dish can be a family staple or served for special occasions and, like many Afghan dishes, is designed to feed many.

In Mr. Jamili's words, "Whenever we get together with friends, with people like you, it fills the void."

Uzbek Palaw (Traditional Afghan Pilaf with Meat)

Serves 8 (makes about 16 cups)

NOTE: Plan ahead as the rice needs to soak for at least 3 hours. Golden Sella rice is available in some supermarkets, as well as Indian specialty markets and online. The *palaw* spices are available at Penzeys, Indian specialty markets, and online, or you can make them yourself (see recipe). You will be using a total of 2 tablespoons of the combined spices once they are ground together.

- 2½ cups Golden Sella rice (see Note)
- Cumin seeds (see Note)
- Green cardamom seeds (see Note)
- Black cardamom seeds (see Note)
- ¾ cup sesame oil
- 3 medium onions, thinly sliced
- About 1¼ pound meat (veal, beef, or lamb), cut into bite-sized pieces
- 1½ tablespoons salt
- 1 teaspoon granulated sugar
- ½ cup raisins, or more for garnish, optional
- 3 carrots, peeled and cut into thin matchsticks (about 1½ cups)

TO PREPARE THE RICE: Rinse the rice with cold water. Soak the rice in water for 3 hours, or overnight.

TO MAKE THE *PALAW* SPICE BLEND: Use a food processor, blender, or a mortar and pestle to combine equal amounts of cumin seeds, green cardamom seeds, and black cardamom seeds, and grind them finely. Set aside 2 tablespoons of the mixture and store the remainder for future use.

TO MAKE *UZBEK PALAW*: In a large, oven-proof pot over medium heat, warm the sesame oil. Add the onions and cook for 5 minutes. Add the meat, salt, sugar and 1 tablespoon of the *palaw* spice mixture. Stir to coat and then cook for 10 minutes.

Add 2 cups water to the pot, cover, and cook for another 30 minutes. Add the raisins and carrots and cook for 3 more minutes.

Preheat the oven to 450°F. Strain the rice and spread it on top of the meat-carrots mixture. Add 1¾ cups more water to the pot, increase the heat and bring the mixture to a boil for 10 minutes. Sprinkle the remaining 1 tablespoon *palaw* spices over the rice and, using the handle of a spoon, poke the rice a few times to make room for evaporation. Cover the pot and transfer it to the oven for 20 minutes. If the rice isn't soft enough, reduce the oven temperature to 300°F and bake for an additional 10 minutes.

TO SERVE: Spoon the rice layer from the pot and spread it on a platter. Then remove the meat, carrots, and raisins, layering them over the rice. Garnish with additional raisins (optional). Serve hot.

Uzbek Palaw

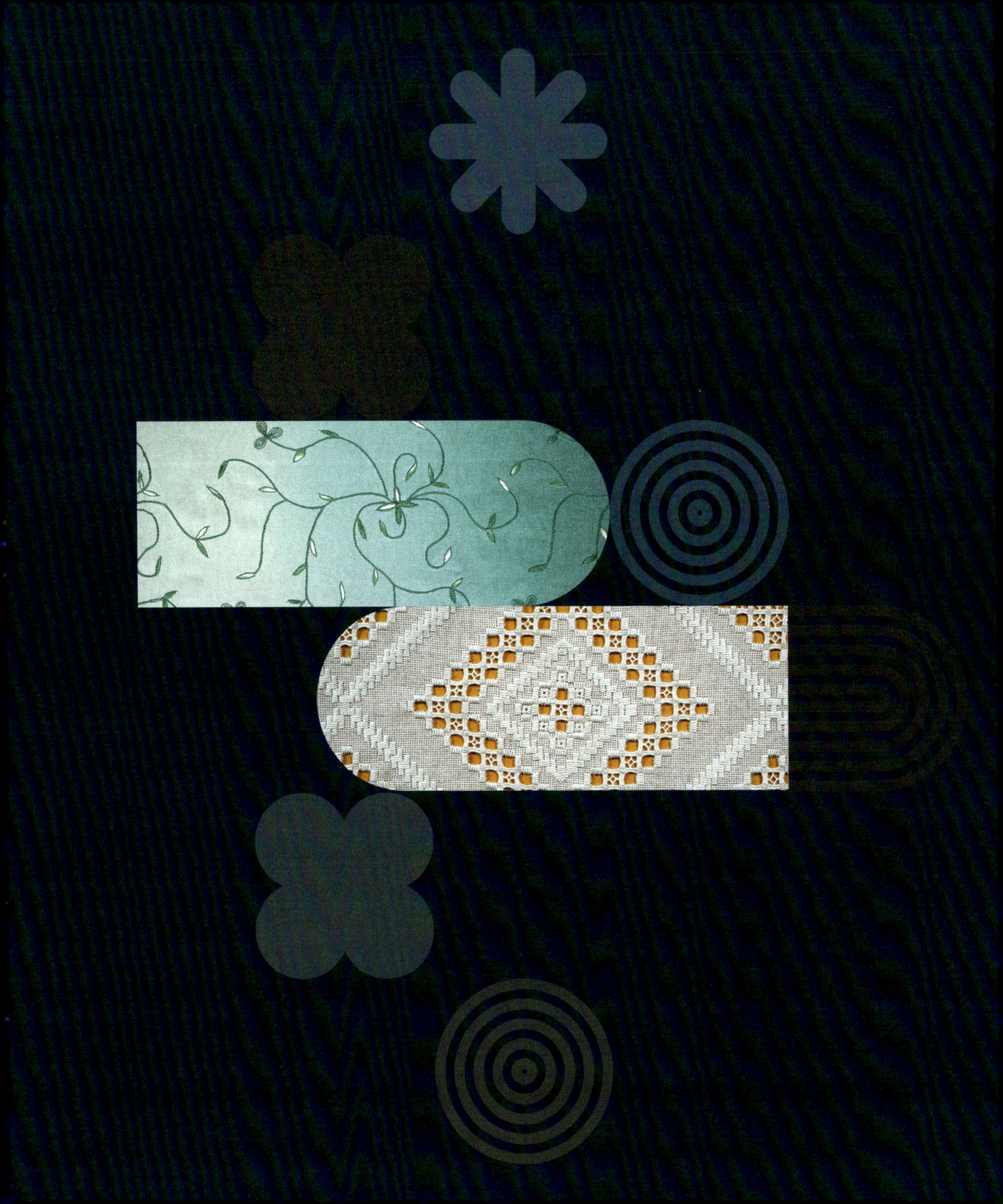

KITCHENS OF OPPORTUNITY

The glimmer of opportunity motivates many immigrants. That was true for Rashmi Bhattachan, who grew up in a family of noteworthy cooks in Nepal and who later became the owner of several Minnesota restaurants. The Sankhu Palubari Community School in Nepal, founded in 1999 by the Advocates for Human Rights, offers opportunity by educating students for the world. As a child in Belarus, Alena Levina wanted to be a translator and travel the world, which she did when she moved to the United States with her family. Alya Jawaid, born in the United States and raised in Pakistan, returned to the United States for a medical residency and stayed. Thekla Rura-Polley left Germany to earn graduate degrees, becoming an immigrant in two countries. Stine Aasland departed Norway for a country where she could pursue her entrepreneurial dreams. Margaret McLean spent her early years in Ukraine, then moved to Arizona with her parents when her mother found employment there. These newcomers to the United States were not the only recipients of opportunity, however. So were the communities they joined, who reaped the benefits of those who brought skills, enthusiasm, traditions, and new foods to neighborhoods and beyond.

RASHMI BHATTACHAN

NEPAL

Rashmi Bhattachan was destined to be a restaurateur. Born in central Nepal, in Pokhara, a gateway to a popular trail in the Himalayas, she grew up in a family where food and hospitality were central. Her mother and two grandmothers were excellent cooks. Her aunt ran a famous hotel near Kathmandu, feeding and entertaining guests. At age twelve, Rashmi learned how to cook from those women, who instilled in her the motto for her life's work: *Atithidevo bhava* ("Treat guests as gods").

Rashmi moved to the United States in 1997 to pursue higher education, earning an undergraduate degree in human resources management and a master's degree in business administration. She received her green card (permanent residency to live and work in the United States) and then launched her first business, a food stand at the Mill City Farmers Market in downtown Minneapolis. That's where she introduced Minnesotans to *momos* (filled dumplings) and earned the nickname "the Momo Lady."

Her food stand was a stepping stone to opening Gorkha Palace in 2010 with chef and fellow Nepali, Sarala Kattel. The Minneapolis restaurant is named after a historical palace that sits atop a hill in Nepal, from where snow-capped mountains can be seen. Three other restaurants followed: MomoDosa at the Market at Malcolm Yards and Midtown Global Market, both in Minneapolis, along with Thaliwala Kitchen in Chanhassen. Her restaurants offer farm-to-table foods that reflect the flavors of the Himalayas, from the *momos* of Tibet to the flavorful curries of Nepal and India.

She measures her success by the support she has received from customers over many years, a sure sign that she continues to live her motto. She loves to see customers who are not of Nepalese heritage dining at her restaurants. "It's humbling to see them enjoying foods they didn't grow up with," she says.

Community is a focus for both Rashmi and her restaurants. She and her husband helped found the Association of Nepalis in Minnesota, devoted to preserving and promoting an active and supportive community among Nepalis and friends of Nepal in Minnesota. Her future goals include a global nongovernmental organization serving the disabled community in Nepal. This reflects the poor nutrition and hazardous conditions for child labor there that have led to large numbers of physical disabilities. She dreams of using sales of her fermented pickles to help fund a bus for the disabled.

Rashmi shares her family recipe for *Chyau Tarkari*, a mushroom curry served with potatoes, that is on the menu at Gorkha Palace. Relatively quick and simple to make, it is a savory introduction to Nepal.

Rashmi Bhattachan

Chyau Tarkari (Mushroom Curry with Potatoes)

Serves 2 to 3

About 1 pound Russet potatoes, unpeeled

2 tablespoons cooking oil

¼ teaspoon ground turmeric

½ teaspoon ground cumin

½ teaspoon ground coriander

¼ teaspoon timur peppercorns, crushed (see Note)

2 cups oyster or button mushrooms, wiped clean and kept whole or sliced, as preferred

Thai chile pepper or hotter chile, seeded and chopped, optional

2 garlic cloves, minced

2 dashes freshly squeezed lemon juice

1 tomato, optional

NOTE: Timur peppercorns (also known as timut peppercorns) have a citrusy spice flavor that makes your tongue tingle. Whole Foods carries these; they are also available online. Sichuan peppercorns are similar, with a stronger numbing sensation.

Cut the potatoes into strips like French fries. Heat the oil in a medium-sized pan on low heat, and add the turmeric, sautéing briefly. Add the potatoes to the pan, and sauté on low heat for about 5 minutes. Add the cumin, coriander, and a pinch of timur to the pan, and sauté another 5 to 10 minutes, until the potatoes are half-cooked (total cooking time for half-cooked potatoes is about 12 minutes).

Add the mushrooms to the pan and sauté for another 15 minutes. If you want a spicier dish, add a Thai chile or an extra-hot chile pepper. Stir occasionally, scraping the bottom of the pan to keep the spices from sticking too much.

When the potatoes are almost done cooking, add the garlic and lemon juice. Add another pinch of timur for extra flavor, if you prefer.

OPTION: Rashmi serves this dish "dry," meaning without gravy. If you prefer gravy, grate one tomato over a bowl to catch the juice and pulp, discarding the skin that remains attached to the stem end. Add the tomato's juice and pulp when the mushrooms are combined with the potatoes.

timur peppercorns

Chyau Tarkari

SANKHU PALUBARI COMMUNITY SCHOOL

NEPAL

The sound of children's laughter can be heard in the Kathmandu Valley of Nepal where 375 children gather in the Sankhu Palubari Community School (SPCS). Founded by the Advocates for Human Rights in 1999, the school provides free, high-quality education and a daily meal to pre-K through tenth grade students, regardless of caste or ethnicity. The Advocates operates SPCS in partnership with the local community and Educate the Children-Nepal.

While public education in Nepal is technically free, the cost of supplies and school fees present a significant financial barrier for many Nepali families,

Students at the Sankhu Palubari Community School

Students at the Sankhu Palubari Community School

forcing them to send their children to work instead of school. Child labor remains widespread in Nepal, with an estimated 1.1 million children from ages 5 to 15 participating in some form of child labor.

One of these children could have been Ashmita. Born in the Kathmandu Valley to a low-income family, she was more likely to spend her childhood working and caring for her younger siblings than graduating from school. Instead, through SPCS, where 53 percent of the student body are girls, Ashmita was able to receive a free education. Seizing this opportunity, Ashmita excelled in her studies and graduated from SPCS, allowing her to pursue a secondary education and complete a master's degree in finance. Ashmita has since returned to SPCS as a teacher, committed to ensuring the same educational opportunities are available for all the children in her community.

Parbati also made use of the opportunities available to her at SPCS. As a child, she lived in a three-room home with her parents and younger brother. She began her studies at SPCS when she was eight years old. A curious and bright student, Parbati was interviewed by the Advocates when she was in the sixth grade, where she shared her dream to become a doctor. Parbati was an excellent student—math was her favorite subject—graduating from SPCS in 2017 with the district's highest score on the national standardized test. Parbati has continued to pursue her childhood dream and is now enrolled in medical school. These two students demonstrate the value of giving a child the opportunity to thrive. Through their education at SPCS, Ashmita and Parbati have been able to pursue their dreams, find success, and give back to their communities.

A traditional dish in Nepal, often served for lunch at the school, is *dal bhat*, a lentil curry with rice. This recipe is a gift from the school community.

Dal Bhat (Nepali Lentils and Rice)

Serves 4

2 tablespoons ghee or cooking oil (see Note)

1 onion, diced

2 garlic cloves, minced

2-inch piece of ginger root, peeled and grated or finely minced (about 2 tablespoons), or 1 teaspoon ground ginger

1 teaspoon coriander seeds, crushed, or 1 teaspoon ground coriander

½ teaspoon ground cayenne pepper

½ teaspoon ground turmeric

1 cup red lentils, rinsed (see Note)

1 teaspoon salt

2 tablespoons freshly chopped cilantro

Cooked white rice

NOTE: Ghee is clarified butter, which is widely available ready-made in supermarkets. Red lentils turn yellow when cooked.

Heat the ghee or oil in a large frying pan over medium-high heat. Add the onions and cook until translucent. Reduce the heat to low and add the garlic, ginger root, coriander, cayenne pepper, and turmeric. Cook, stirring, about 3 minutes.

Add the red lentils to the onion mixture and stir to combine. Add 3 cups water, cover, and bring to a boil. Add the salt, reduce the heat to very low and cook until the lentils are tender, about 15 minutes. Remove from the heat and stir in the cilantro. Serve with the cooked rice.

red lentils

Dal Bhat

ALENA LEVINA
BELARUS

Although Alena Levina has been in the United States for more than twenty years after emigrating from Belarus, she's still surprised by the sense of freedom that citizenship offers. "With an American passport, people don't necessarily understand the freedom, but you can travel almost anywhere," says Alena. "In Belarus, you need to get visas for everywhere, and sometimes you just can't go."

She and her husband immigrated to the United States along with her husband's family. "His grandmother moved here, then the whole rest of the family moved together," she says. This was after earlier immigrations of family members in the 1970s and 1980s. Alena's parents followed after her own children were born. "I sponsored my parents," she says. The benefit of family extended to mealtime. "My kids grew up with their grandmothers' cooking."

Long before she arrived in the United States, Alena dreamed of becoming an interpreter, and of traveling the world. "In America, this dream came true," she says. She became a volunteer translator for the Advocates for Human Rights and translates for Russian speakers for official court documents as well as more informal discussions. "There's just so much opportunity in America," Alena says. "That was so surprising to me and provided so much strength." She switched careers from finance to IT, now working as a senior systems developer for Capella University.

Food back in Belarus was shaped by the climate, which is often harsh, with cold summers. This was weather that suited potatoes, carrots, cabbage, and beets, which found a place at dinner tables throughout the country. In her family home in Belarus, they did not have a car and had only a small refrigerator. Wanting to extend vitamins through the winter, they canned provisions and stored them in a cellar. Beets, easy to grow and to prepare for meals, became a staple in the form of borscht.

She shares a favorite recipe for summer beet soup, called *holodnik*, which means "cold soup." "As a mother, I think the biggest goal with the recipe is to put as many vegetables as you can, right?" she says. "It's the ultimate international mother's goal." She gathers her vegetables at the farmers market and through Community Supported Agriculture shares. "I think the majority of my friends are from Ukraine, Belarus, and Russia, so we kind of cook those things in the kitchen," she says. "We all have recipes we make from our childhood. I've definitely gotten a lot of compliments cooking traditional recipes."

Alena Levina

Holodnik (Summer Beet Soup)

Serves 6

NOTE: Plan ahead because this soup definitely improves if it is refrigerated for at least several hours before serving. Hard-cook the eggs in advance, if using for a garnish. For the cucumbers, peel the skins if they are too thick. Alena suggests that small cucumbers with thinner skins, usually available only at farmers markets, are preferred. "They're so crunchy, I feel like they make this dish better."

- 3 to 4 eggs, for garnish
- 1½ pounds red beets (3 large or 8 small)
- 1 quart plain, whole-milk kefir, or buttermilk
- 2 teaspoons salt
- 1 teaspoon granulated sugar
- 1 small onion or 3 green onions, thinly sliced
- 1 bunch fresh dill, chopped, or 1 tablespoon dried, and more fresh dill for garnish
- 3 to 4 small cucumbers, diced (1½ to 2 cups; see Note)
- Sour cream, radishes, or croutons, for garnish

TO MAKE HARD-COOKED EGGS: Place the eggs in a small pan, cover with water, and bring to a boil over medium-high heat. Remove the pan from the heat, cover the pan, and let sit for 15 minutes. Drain the water and add cold water, repeating until the eggs have cooled. Refrigerate until ready to use.

TO MAKE THE SOUP: Scrub the beets and cut off the greens (you can save the greens for another dish). Place the beets in a pot, cover them generously with water, and bring to a boil over medium-high heat. Cook the beets until just soft, about 30 to 40 minutes. Drain and discard the water and let the beets cool. To peel them easily, push firmly near the top end of the beet and the skin should slide off. You may want to use kitchen gloves to keep your fingers from getting stained.

In a large bowl or pot, combine the kefir (or buttermilk) with 5 cups water. Grate the beets (there should be about 2 cups) and add to the kefir mixture. Add salt and sugar, then the onions, dill, and cucumbers. Cover and refrigerate for several hours.

TO SERVE THE SOUP: Divide the chilled soup into bowls. Garnish with fresh dill, a dollop of sour cream, radish slices, and/or croutons. Peel the hard-cooked eggs and slice them in half. Garnish each bowl with half of an egg.

Holodnik

ALYA JAWAID

UNITED STATES AND PAKISTAN

Alya Jawaid

Alya Jawaid was born in the United States to a father who had immigrated to California from Pakistan to study civil engineering. Her mother came to the United States from the Philippines as a doctor. When Alya and her sister were young, they moved to their father's country, where they lived with an aunt and uncle who raised the girls as their own. Following in her mother's footsteps, Alya studied medicine in Pakistan, where she met her husband at Aga-khan University Medical School. The couple came to the United States to complete their medical residencies and stayed.

As a child, Alya returned to the United States every summer to visit. This was a big shift for her. In the United States, she stood out a bit. She spoke with an accent, and didn't wear Western clothes all the time, and she missed home. But where was home? Now when she goes back to Pakistan, her thermostat is Minnesotan and her politics have changed, she says. She does not quite fit in either country.

Alya wants her own children to experience both cultures. They love to go to Pakistan, eat the food, travel, and play with their cousins. But they are "purely American," Alya says. They want to look like their peers in the United States. Her son understands Urdu, the family's language from Pakistan, and her daughter would like to learn to speak it. Alya does not want to pressure them or ask them to represent Pakistani culture each time they go out. Yet she wants her children to know they have a rich heritage.

Alya has many skills beyond medicine, including drawing and painting. During the pandemic, she contributed to an exhibit of artwork that honored women of color who were physicians and worked on the front lines providing health care. Now that her children are mostly raised, she has returned to the medical profession herself, opening an internal-medicine practice in Minnesota.

Food serves as a tie to Pakistan for Alya. True to her training as a doctor, she offers a nutritious recipe that serves as comfort food. Called *khichdi* or *khichri* (KITCH-er-ee) this simple dish of rice and lentils is versatile. Alya serves it with some of her favorites: yogurt, pickles, chutney, and a tomato-cucumber salad. "This is the simplest thing I could do that makes me think of home," she says.

Khichdi can be customized in many ways: made more or less spicy, with more or less water, with meat or without. "It's the first food kids are introduced to," Alya says. "The elderly are eating it. It's gluten free; it's vegan. You could dress it up any way you want." Some cooks add kebabs to the dish, and her husband's family adds an omelet on top. A spiced black tea makes a nice finish for the meal.

Khichdi

Khichdi (Lentils and Rice)

Serves 2

NOTE: Plan ahead, as the lentils and rice need to soak for 30 minutes. Moong lentils are also called *moon dal* on some packaging. Garam masala is a spice mixture of at least eight elements, that is widely available.

- ⅓ cup yellow Moong lentils (see Note)
- ⅓ cup basmati rice
- 1 to 2 tablespoons neutral cooking oil or ghee
- ½ onion, thinly sliced
- 1 teaspoon cumin seeds
- Salt, to taste
- ¼ teaspoon ground cumin
- Garam masala, a generous pinch, optional (see Note)
- 1 cup water or chicken stock, plus more as needed

Rinse and soak the lentils and rice together for at least 30 minutes. In the meantime, warm the vegetable oil or ghee in a large pot over medium heat and sauté the onions until soft. Add the cumin seeds and sauté for 30 seconds.

Drain the water from the lentil and rice mixture, and add the mixture to the onions with salt to taste. Add the ground cumin and garam masala, if using. Sauté the mixture for a bit, then add 1 cup water or chicken stock. Bring to a boil. Lower the heat, cover, and let the mixture simmer for 15 to 20 minutes, stirring occasionally. Add more liquid if the mixture is sticking or if the water evaporates before your desired consistency is reached.

When done, serve family-style with a bowl of Greek yogurt, your favorite kind of pickles, mango relish or Green Mint Chutney (see recipe, page 77), and a salad of thinly sliced cucumbers and tomatoes dressed with lemon juice. Cardamom-Infused Tea is a perfect ending for this meal, especially when served with a varied selection of nougat candies.

Green Mint Chutney

Makes about 1 cup

- ½ teaspoon cumin seeds
- 1 bunch fresh mint leaves, stems discarded (about 1 cup)
- 1 bunch fresh cilantro, with stems included (about 1 cup)
- 1 jalapeño, stemmed (may discard the seeds, if desired, for less heat)
- Freshly squeezed juice from 1 lemon
- Salt, to taste
- 1 to 2 garlic cloves

To roast cumin seeds, warm them in a dry pan over low heat until fragrant.

In a blender, process the mint, cilantro, jalapeño, lemon juice, salt, garlic, and cumin seeds until the mixture is smooth and velvety. Taste and adjust the salt and lemon juice as needed. Serve over *Khichdi* or other dishes.

Cardamom-Infused Tea

Serves 2 to 4

- 4 individual tea bags of black tea (Earl Grey works well)
- Cinnamon stick
- 3 to 5 whole cloves
- 3 to 5 cardamom pods
- Cream and sugar, optional

Put the tea bags in a pot with 4 cups water. Add the cinnamon stick, cloves, and cardamom pods, and bring to a boil. Lower the heat and simmer for 10 minutes. Strain and serve each cup of tea with a generous splash of cream and a spoon of sugar, if preferred.

THEKLA RURA-POLLEY

GERMANY

Thekla Rura-Polley came to the United States as a student, planning to return to Germany after her studies. Thirty-three years later, living in the United States, she notes with a laugh that her international moves satisfied two of her life's dreams: to see the Grand Canyon and to hear the world's largest church organ, an instrument she had studied.

Thekla grew up near Dillenburg, in western Germany, a historic town where she attended Wilhelm-von-Oranien-Schule, founded in 1537. After graduating from college, a scholarship offered her the opportunity to study abroad. She remembered a film about the Grand Canyon that she had seen in grade school, which influenced her decision to study in the United States. She landed 1,650 miles east of the Grand Canyon in Madison, Wisconsin, where she earned a master's degree and then a PhD in business administration. While there, she did what most German students in the United States do and traveled five thousand miles visiting national parks: Mount Rushmore, Yellowstone, Grand Teton, Mesa Verde, and yes, the Grand Canyon.

After completing her degrees, she received an email from a professor suggesting a job opportunity. He had been located in Scotland and that appealed to her because it was closer to her home in Germany. However, to her surprise, the professor had relocated to Australia. Ever the adventurer and interested in working with this professor (as well as hearing the world's largest church organ, which at the time was in Sydney), Thekla and her American-born husband packed their bags and moved to Australia.

To ensure that both could work in Australia, they applied for, and received, permanent resident status there. Six years later, and by then the parents of a daughter, they returned to the United States and moved to Minnesota to be closer to her husband's family. Thekla was granted permanent resident alien status in the United States, though her children insist she does not look at all like the typical alien featured in movies. For the past fifteen years, Thekla has focused on development for community and human rights organizations, most recently as director of development for the Advocates for Human Rights.

"The people we see here as clients are the few who were able to leave," she says. "It's 'survivor' bias. They were strong enough to walk for hundreds or even thousands of miles. They may have survived trafficking or whatever happened to them at the borders. They often can draw on their resilience and strength."

As an immigrant in two countries, Thekla affirms their value. "Together we make the community more vibrant, we enlarge the economy, and we enlarge the pie so that everybody can partake of it." Food plays a part. "It's a great contributor to the vibrancy of a community," she says. "Immigration really sparks the creativity and variety of foods."

Her favorite recipe: *Lauchtorte*, or leek tart. This recipe dates back to Thekla's early college days in Germany, when two mentors offered to cook with her and other first-year students and suggested a leek tart. "We all went shopping together and then went back to their apartment and made it together," she says. She continues to make it, serving it with a simple green salad. *Guten appetit!* Enjoy your meal!

Thekla Rura-Polley

Lauchtorte (Leek Tart)

Makes 1 (9-inch) tart, 6 to 8 servings

NOTE: Plan ahead, as the frozen puff pastry needs to be thawed overnight. Instead of puff pastry, you could use your own preferred savory crust. The recipe calls for a 9-inch springform pan. A standard pie pan could be used, but it may be more difficult to get the finished tart out of the pan.

TART SHELL

2 sheets of puff pastry, thawed according to package directions (see Note)

TART FILLING

4 large (or 6 medium) leeks

4 garlic cloves, chopped (or 1 tablespoon minced)

1 tablespoon freshly chopped chives

2 tablespoons freshly chopped flat-leaf parsley, plus more for garnish

1 cup cubed ham (or chopped cooked bacon, minus the fatty parts), optional

EGG MIXTURE

2 eggs

1 cup heavy cream (or half-and-half)

Salt and freshly ground pepper, to taste

Freshly ground nutmeg, to taste

8 ounces shredded cheese, such as Gruyère or Parmesan (any cheese that melts well)

TO MAKE THE TART SHELL: Preheat the oven to 350°F. On a clean work surface, use a rolling pin to gently roll out a sheet of puff pastry to a square that is at least 10 inches wide. Place a 9-inch springform pan in the center of the puff pastry. Using a sharp knife, cut the puff pastry in a circle around the pan, leaving ½ inch around the pan's edge. Line the bottom of the pan with the circle of puff pastry, allowing it to reach up the sides a little. Carefully press the puff pastry into the pan's creases.

Use a rolling pin to gently roll out the second sheet of puff pastry to a long rectangle. Using a sharp knife, cut a rectangle that is slightly longer than the pan's circumference and ½ inch wider than the pan's height. Line the sides of the pan with the puff pastry. Press the connection of the bottom sheet of puff pastry and the side sheet of puff pastry to make a continuous shell for the tart. Make sure there are no holes, to prevent the filling from leaking out. Using a sharp knife, trim any excess puff pastry from the top of the pan. Discard the extra puff pastry or save it for another use.

TO MAKE THE FILLING: Cut the leeks in half lengthwise and rinse thoroughly, removing any sandy grit. Bring a large pot of water to boil over high heat. Blanch the leeks for 30 seconds. Empty the blanched leeks into a colander to drain. Allow the leeks to dry completely, then chop them into ¼- to ½-inch pieces. Transfer the chopped leeks to a large bowl. Add the garlic, chives, and parsley, and mix to combine. Add the cubed ham (or chopped bacon, optional), and mix to combine.

TO MAKE THE EGG MIXTURE: In a medium bowl, whisk the eggs until they are uniform in color. Add the heavy cream, salt, pepper, and nutmeg, and whisk to combine.

TO ASSEMBLE THE TART: Spread the leeks evenly over the puff pastry. Pour the egg mixture over the leeks. Top with an even layer of the

Lauchtorte

shredded cheese. Place the springform pan on a rimmed baking sheet and bake until the filling is firm, about 1 hour. Remove the tart from the oven and set it on a wire rack to cool for 5 minutes. To serve, remove the tart from the springform pan and transfer it to a platter. Garnish with thyme or chopped parsley and serve with a simple green salad.

STINE AASLAND

NORWAY

Stine Aasland

Stine Aasland headed to the United States in 2015 because of its food. Or rather, because of a food the country lacked: Nordic-style waffles. These are thin, firmer versions of the American staple, made in heart shapes, that are easy to fold, sandwich-style, over fillings.

Today the entrepreneur from Telemark, Norway, is the founder of Nordic Waffles, based in Minnesota, with frozen and fresh waffles in supermarkets and food service locations. Hers was a dream based on scale: A Norwegian population of 5.5 million, compared to 332 million in the United States (2021 figures). That added up to opportunity for her.

In Norway, waffles are more snack than breakfast staple. They're traditionally served cold, often packed in school lunch boxes and available in convenience stores, including gas stations, which tend to have fresh foods available. At age twenty-one, Stine bought into a Norwegian gas station franchise and introduced her waffles there, which were made with premium ingredients. Four years later she sold that franchise and started a waffle factory, bringing the snack to parks, amusement areas, and stores around her country—700 venues—all the while breaking Norwegian waffle rules by introducing a different batter and unpredictable fillings.

But Stine wanted more. And that's when she sold her shares in the company, packed her bags and waffle maker, and headed to the United States to create a North American waffle empire. Stine traveled the country alone, from the East Coast to California and everywhere in between, checking out the waffle world. On the West Coast, she stopped at the Culinary Arts Institute and learned that every country has its own flavor profile, and in the United States that meant cinnamon, cream cheese, and bacon, critical information for a waffle maker.

A visit to Minneapolis brought a chance stop at the bright blue Norway House, where she made connections and found support that led her to the Center for Innovation at the University of North Dakota in Grand Forks. There she got hands-on business lessons and perfected her waffle batter. Then it was back to Minneapolis where she began creating a following by introducing the waffles at coffeehouses, where they were made to order. One waffle led to another, and her venture expanded to event catering and, eventually, to the Minnesota State Fair, where she found an enthusiastic clientele and raves from critics.

And then the pandemic hit. Stine had already been thinking about how to expand her business with a frozen product. This was the time. Americans, she found, were open to new foods—and new versions of traditional foods—much more so than Norwegians, who expected every waffle to taste like their mother's.

"I've always known what my vision was," she says. "I came to America to create a 'wafflelution,' to be the leading waffle brand in the United States. It's a bold plan and part of why I left Norway. The United States was big and so interesting to me, with so many people." Those people, she found, did not mind a waffle batter different from the usual.

At first, she was confused by business laws, which she assumed would be the same all over the country. Then she realized that every state had its own regulations. And she found that, as an entrepreneur, she couldn't fulfill that dream on her own. "You need people better than you," she says. "There's so much you don't know in business." She found that she had to adapt to the American taste palate. "That's Rule Number 1," she says.

Rule Number 2 is the culture of cooking, a tough lesson she learned on the plains of North Dakota when she started up her first waffle location at a gas station. Given the novelty of her enterprise and the local press she received, eighty people showed up the day she opened. And then the business died off.

"I needed to adapt to American culture, which is always going to be convenience, especially in a fast-food market," she says. "It doesn't mean you can't have new innovative products, but it can't be too hard to understand." Her mistake in North Dakota? Serving the waffles cold, with brown cheese, just as she would have done in Norway. No cinnamon, cream cheese, or bacon. She learned her lesson. Today Stine sells Nordic Waffles in supermarkets nationwide, filling them with cinnamon, cream cheese, bacon, and other popular ingredients. It is a "waffleution" after all.

Norwegian Waffles

Makes about 14 waffles

Recipe from We Love Waffles: The Heart of Scandinavian Culture, *by Stine Aasland.*

NOTE: Plan ahead, as the batter needs to rest for at least 15 minutes. These waffles are much thinner and firmer than those found in most American recipes. The batter can be refrigerated for up to 5 days or frozen for later use. For Scandinavian effect, use a waffle maker that produces thin, heart-shaped waffles. Cinnamon sugar is easy to make, with equal amounts of ground cinnamon and granulated sugar.

½ teaspoon salt
4 cups flour
2 teaspoons ground cardamom
4 cups whole milk
¾ cup sour cream
3 eggs
½ cup granulated sugar
¾ cup (1½ sticks) butter, melted

In a medium bowl, whisk together the salt, flour, and cardamom, and set aside.

In a medium bowl, combine the milk and sour cream, and whisk until thoroughly combined, and set aside.

In the bowl of an electric mixer on medium speed, beat the eggs and sugar until light and frothy. Reduce the speed to low. Add part of the flour mixture to the egg/sugar mixture, then add part of the milk mixture, and mix until incorporated. Alternate with more additions until it is all combined. Increase the speed to medium and beat until the batter is smooth, about 3 minutes. Reduce the speed to low. Slowly add the melted butter to the batter, mixing until thoroughly incorporated. Let the batter rest for at least 15 minutes before making waffles.

Preheat the waffle maker and proceed with the batter as appliance directions specify. A 12-inch griddle uses about ½ cup batter. Serve with any toppings: berries, whipped cream, cinnamon sugar (see Note). Or do as Stine does in her Nordic Waffles enterprise: Fold the waffles in half and stuff them with interesting flavor combinations.

Norwegian Waffles

MARGARET McLEAN

UKRAINE

Margaret's story begins in Kyiv, Ukraine, where she was born Margarita Vadimovna Smoylovskaya. Her mother, Nadia, was a "girl who codes," long before it was a thing to do; and that is what brought the family to the United States. A textile engineer by training, Nadia pivoted early in her career to learn computer programming, skills she used to develop and manage complex modeling frameworks. With very little refrigeration available in Ukraine, milk, bread, and vegetables were sold fresh in small neighborhood stores, and computer models were critical to make sure that food arrived where it was needed, and only in the amounts that were likely to be consumed.

In the early 1970s, Nadia was one of three women attending an international conference on nonmilitary computer applications. A faculty member at the University of Arizona, who was in the audience, convinced the university to petition the Soviets to allow Nadia to teach a seminar to interest women in computing. Sensing a propaganda opportunity, the Soviet government agreed, and Nadia and her family landed in Tucson, Arizona, in 1976.

At thirteen, speaking no English, Margarita found herself in what felt like a small town, in the middle of a scorching summer. "I think transition would have been very traumatic if I knew that I was leaving everything behind, as many immigrants do," she says. "Instead, I was going on a 'grand adventure' for just a few months, and it did not seem like a big deal, at the time."

A few months later, when the family decided to stay, Margarita, now Margaret, had friends at school and enjoyed freedoms that teenagers did not have back home. Her English was improving rapidly. While her mother worked on lesson plans for complex computer networks, Margaret assisted at a kindergarten camp. "Working with little kids is a great way to learn a foreign language," Margaret reminisces. "They use simple phrases and are brutal when you mispronounce words. You never make the same mistake twice!"

After graduating from high school at sixteen, Margaret attended the University of Arizona on full scholarship, later earning a master of business administration degree in finance while employed at Hewlett Packard. After working in IT for several years, she went to law school. As a partner in a law firm, she returned to Kyiv to open an office there, and later became general counsel of a global engineering company that managed the construction of a sarcophagus to enclose the exploded reactor at the Chernobyl nuclear plant, located not very far from Kyiv. Full circle, it would seem. Today she works in the United States serving as the general counsel and chief risk officer for a large technology company with operations in twenty-one countries.

Margaret grew up without learning how to cook. Most of what she knows about Ukrainian cooking came from her daughter's Ukrainian nanny, who helped recreate old recipes Margaret remembered from family meals, using modern American ingredients. The dish here, *pirozhki* (a filled pastry) adopts the use of commercial biscuit dough. *Pirozhkis* are eaten as a snack or appetizer or, as Margaret did in Ukraine, as a bread with soup or dessert. She often brings them to American Christmas cookie exchanges, where they are very popular.

Margaret McLean

Pirozhki (Ukrainian Buns with Filling)

Makes 10

1 tablespoon butter or olive oil

½ onion, chopped (about ¼ cup)

½ small jalapeño, seeded and diced, or about ¼ cup diced green bell pepper, or ½ (4-ounce) can of diced chiles (see Note)

½ pound ground beef

Salt and pepper, to taste

Buttermilk biscuit dough for 10 biscuits

Flour, for rolling dough

1 egg, beaten

NOTE: In the Ukraine, the dough for these filled buns is made by scratch, but in the United States, Margaret substitutes commercially made refrigerated biscuit dough. She uses the regular-size biscuit dough, not the large size. Margaret prefers to add a little heat with green chiles to the traditional recipe, specifically the chopped version in a can. Fresh bell peppers or hot peppers could be used as a substitute. You will need a pastry brush.

Preheat the oven to 375°F. In a large pan, melt the butter (or heat the olive oil) over medium heat, and sauté the onion slowly until it caramelizes a bit. Add the chile pepper (or green bell pepper) and cook until softened (if using canned chiles, wait before adding them). Add the ground beef to the pan and brown thoroughly. If using canned chile peppers, drain them and add at this time to warm them up. Remove the pan from the heat and drain off any fat.

Line a baking sheet with parchment paper. Spread a little flour thinly on a counter and break open the biscuit dough. Using a lightly floured rolling pin or your fingers, roll or stretch the biscuits one at a time to form circles about 3½ inches in diameter. Place the circles of dough on the prepared baking sheet about 2 inches apart. Put about 2 tablespoons filling in the center of each biscuit, evenly distributing the meat.

Dip your fingers in a small bowl of water and run them around the outside edge of each biscuit. This will help seal the edges. Fold each biscuit in half to create a crescent shape with the filling inside. Press the exterior edges together tightly (you may need to dab a bit more water between the edges if the dough doesn't cooperate). Press each biscuit firmly on the parchment paper so the bottom of the biscuit is flat.

Using a pastry brush, coat each biscuit with the beaten egg. Bake until nicely brown, about 10 to 12 minutes, watching closely at the end so the biscuits don't get too dark.

Alternative Ukrainian fillings for the rolls: Mashed potatoes with caramelized onions. Or stewed cabbage. Or use sweet fillings, such as sour cherries or peaches.

Pirozhki

KITCHENS OF JUSTICE

All human beings are born free and equal in dignity and rights.

—Article 1, The Universal Declaration of Human Rights, United Nations, December 10, 1948

The wheels of justice may move slowly, but they also dip into the kitchen. Nadia Najarro Smith, who was a lawyer in Guatemala and defended human rights, today serves as a court interpreter and translator in Minnesota. Mehmet Türkoğlu, a lawyer in Turkey, came to the University of Minnesota to study human rights and stayed when a coup developed in his homeland. Deegii Lkhasuren left Mongolia to study human rights in Minnesota. Olga Baranova moved to the United States from Russia to protect herself and family. Verónica Cadavid González, a Colombian lawyer, came to Minnesota to study human rights. Stephanie Willman Bordat took a different approach. She studied law in the United States and in Paris, then took her skills and interest in human rights to Morocco. All found that food opens another way to connect communities with justice.

NADIA NAJARRO SMITH

GUATEMALA

Nadia Najarro Smith had a lot to live up to. She was born in Guatemala City, Guatemala, to Leticia Najarro, a legendary leader in the labor movement of that country. Leticia was a fierce advocate for farm, factory, and health care workers, organizing hundreds of unions and fighting to improve pay and working conditions for generations of Guatemalan workers. She also worked on initiatives with the presidents in Latin America and the United States and represented workers at the International Labour Organization in Geneva, Switzerland.

Like her mother, Nadia was destined to defend human rights. She enrolled in law school and attended Universidad Rafael Landivar in Guatemala City. She was one of twelve women in her class to graduate. Following graduation in 1981, she took an entry-level position at the judiciary and quickly moved up in the ranks. When the U.S. Department of Justice came to Guatemala, she was one of the staff trained by them. Nadia was further educated in international human rights in Costa Rica before returning to the Guatemalan courts, where she was part of the staff for a Supreme Court department.

Nadia Najarro Smith

Shortly thereafter, an event occurred that changed Nadia's career path. In 1986, protesters gathered in Guatemala City and marched to the Supreme Court to highlight the thousands of people who had been forcibly "disappeared" during the decades-old civil war. Nadia's work as a chief of staff of a criminal court was quickly restructured to create a special tribunal directed to search for those who had been forcibly taken.

This was an enormous challenge for Nadia. She started the tribunal from scratch at a time in the 1980s when resources were scarce. Her massive search was conducted without computers, with typed reports and carbon copies attached to physical files. The tribunal searched everywhere for the missing, from military locations to cemeteries to the ocean. It developed evidence that implicated the army. Many eyes from around the globe watched the tribunal—human rights groups and other organizations. The tribunal was pushed to do more. The Advocates for Human Rights also weighed in and a group of U.S. judges and lawyers came to Guatemala to review the court's progress. They had learned of Nadia's work and shared more names of people who needed to be found. In Nadia's words, the members of the tribunal worked with their "hearts and souls." But as the tribunal continued for more than eighteen months, information became harder to gather, and political endorsement wore thin. Her resources diminished as the interest in justice lessened.

Still, Nadia continued to work in the law, teaching at the university and becoming executive director of the Central American and Caribbean Bar Association, which is a subsidiary of the American Bar Association. She also reconnected with a lawyer from the Advocates, Louis Smith, whom she had met earlier through the tribunal and who was now back in Guatemala. In 1990, Nadia moved to Minnesota on a fiancée visa, and she and Louis married. Nadia studied English and trained as a Spanish language court interpreter and translator, where she continues to serve legal and community constituents, including the labor movement.

Immigration is always hard, with family, friends, and traditions far away. Nadia has now spent more time in Minnesota than in Guatemala, but she still does not feel that she fully belongs. "Inside everyone who leaves their country, there is a sad part, for the irreplaceable pieces that have been left behind, but we are also grateful for the opportunities," she says. Involvement through her work in the Latino community helped her. "It filled the emptiness of being an immigrant," she says.

Food also makes a difference. "It is one way to remember country, land, friends, and family," says Nadia. "Food is a way to connect deeply and a way to belong." When she first came to the United States, she missed Guatemalan food and did not know how to cook. A friend gave her a cookbook, *False Tongues and Sunday Bread: A Guatemalan and Mayan Cookbook*, by Copeland Marks, as a gift when she was pregnant with her daughter. She has since shared this cookbook with her two grown children, and they insisted that she share here the recipe for *Jocón*, one of their favorites.

decorative
Guatemalan box

Jocón (Chicken and Tomatillo Stew)

Serves 4

From False Tongues and Sunday Bread: A Guatemalan and Mayan Cookbook, *by Copeland Marks*

- 1 (3-pound) chicken, cut into serving pieces, loose skin and fat discarded
- 1 teaspoon salt, or to taste
- 2 flour tortillas, sliced in ribbons
- 1 tablespoon pepitas (raw pumpkin seeds)
- ½ cup sesame seeds
- 1 cup freshly chopped cilantro, packed
- 1 cup sliced green onions, green parts only
- ½ cup sliced tomatillos
- 1 to 2 teaspoons roughly chopped hot green chile pepper
- 1 tablespoon vegetable oil
- Cooked white rice and tortillas, for serving

Put the chicken, 4 cups water, and the salt in a covered pot over medium heat and cook for about 30 minutes. Remove the chicken and set aside. Set the chicken broth aside and soak the tortillas in it for about 10 minutes.

Toast the pepitas and sesame seeds in a dry skillet over low to medium heat until they turn a light tan color, about 10 minutes.

In a food processor or blender, grind the pepitas and sesame seeds. Add the cilantro, green onions, tomatillos, chile pepper, and 1 cup of the reserved chicken broth. Add the soaked tortillas and process to a smooth paste.

Brown the chicken pieces in oil in a skillet over medium heat for 5 minutes. Add the green sauce and the remainder of the chicken broth, about 2 cups. Simmer over low heat for 15 minutes, until the sauce is reduced to a thick, rich green consistency. Serve the chicken and sauce warm over rice, with tortillas.

tomatillos

Jocón

MEHMET TÜRKOĞLU

TURKEY

Mehmet Türkoğlu grew up in a world of ethnic discrimination in Turkey, and now is committed to creating change for himself and others. His childhood was spent in eastern Turkey, near the Iranian and Armenian borders. His father's education had ended after elementary school, when he had to earn money for his family. This loss fueled his father's passion for education and his determination to educate his own children, all four of whom went on to attend university. When Mehmet was eight years old, his family moved to western Turkey to access better educational opportunities.

The move from eastern to western Turkey was dramatic in many ways. Health care and education that had been limited in the east were vastly superior in the west. But Mehmet's family had a hard time finding a house to rent, which Mehmet now realizes was due to their ethnicity—Kurdish, the largest minority in Turkey (20 percent of the country's population).

Following high school, Mehmet attended Istanbul University, where he was introduced to human rights law. He recalls feeling mesmerized,

Mehmet Türkoğlu

poring through massive texts to understand human rights movements around the world and the sacrifices people made to affect change. He realized that Kurdish people had to fight to gain access to the most basic human rights, such as the ability to speak in their native language. From 1923 to 1991, a mandate had forbidden Kurdish language in schools, organizations, and publications.

Mehmet's studies led him to work at the Istanbul Bar Association Human Rights Center and later to obtain a master's degree in human rights, after which he landed an academic position in human rights law at the Suleyman Demirel University.

His studies were not only academic, but personal, as he began to understand his own story, the discrimination he experienced as a Kurdish minority in Turkey, and the insidious nature of prejudice. His education opened his eyes to other vulnerable people who quietly suffer discrimination. All of these forces shaped Mehmet's ideas and his commitment to be a voice for human rights. As an academic, Mehmet came to Minnesota in 2016 with a plan to spend the summer working with professor Fionnuala Ní Aoláin at the University of Minnesota, who is both a human rights lawyer and special rapporteur (an independent expert) for the United Nations. One month later, hostilities erupted in Turkey after an attempted military coup, which resulted in the end of the rule of law, freedom of speech, and academic freedom. Mehmet decided to stay in the United States.

He is working to create a new life here while following his passions: human rights and immigration law. Mehmet has worked as a law clerk at a Twin Cities law firm focusing on immigration law, and volunteers at the Advocates for Human Rights. He has drafted multiple reports to the United Nations about human rights practices in Turkey and assisted clients with asylum applications and interviews.

Menemen is the dish that reminds Mehmet of home. "A perfect meal, delicious and easy to cook," he says. "*Menemen* is for everyone." It's a simple meal made of eggs, tomato, green pepper, and spices, and can be eaten any time of day. Traditionally, *menemen* is served for breakfast in a pan placed in the middle of the table where all eat together. It's often accompanied by soft, crusty Turkish bread (similar to a French baguette), olives, feta or Cheddar cheese, honey, and *kaymak* (similar to clotted cream or crème fraîche). There is a friendly controversy in Turkey as to whether *menemen* should be made with or without onion. Mehmet prefers the addition of onion.

Menemen (Vegetables with Eggs)

Serves 4

- 1 to 2 tablespoons olive oil or butter
- 1 green bell pepper (or jalapeño or other hot chile pepper), stemmed, seeded, and diced
- ½ onion, thinly diced, optional
- 2 tomatoes, diced
- 4 eggs
- Shredded mozzarella cheese for topping, optional
- Salt and crushed red pepper flakes
- Freshly ground black pepper and paprika, optional
- Freshly chopped flat-leaf parsley, for garnish

Heat oil or butter in a frying pan. Add the green bell pepper (or hot pepper) and onion (optional) and cook, stirring occasionally, until softened.

Add the diced tomato and continue to stir for a few minutes. Cover the pan and cook for a short time until some, but not all, of the tomatoes' juice evaporates.

Crack the eggs on top of the tomatoes. (If you wish, scramble the whites, or let them be.) Cover the pan to steam the yolks to a desired consistency. For extra flavor, sprinkle mozzarella cheese (optional) across the eggs and let sit a minute to melt.

Season with salt and crushed pepper, to taste. Sprinkle black pepper or paprika on top of the eggs (optional). Garnish with parsley. Serve with warm bread that is crusty on the outside and soft on the inside, along with olives, feta or Cheddar cheese, honey, and *kaymak* (similar to clotted cream or crème fraîche).

crushed red pepper flakes

Menemen

DELGERMAA (DEEGII) LKHASUREN
MONGOLIA

Delgermaa (Deegii) Lkhasuren

Deegii Lkhasuren grew up in Mongolia, close to the Russian border. Although her parents were influenced heavily by Russian culture, they felt it would be beneficial for her to learn English, which she began at a young age. “You don’t just learn the language,” she says. “It comes with the culture. It comes with connections. Your mindset is changed.”

English opened doors for Deegii. Having spent her whole life studying the language, she wanted to live where it was spoken. With a college degree in international relations from a Mongolian school, Deegii applied for many scholarships to support her effort. Ultimately, she obtained a Fulbright scholarship, which took her to the University of Minnesota to earn a master’s degree in public policy. At the completion of the degree, she and her husband had a five-year-old and an infant. They returned to Mongolia, where she began working for Save the Children. “It was a project that really empowered people,” she says.

Later, when she worked for a youth empowerment project, she interacted with young people who were deaf. Mongolia had not fully integrated special-needs children into the educational system and the country's society had essentially ignored them. While she was in Mongolia, the children at a school for the deaf protested peacefully, yet powerfully, with the most basic demands: to be taught by teachers who knew sign language so the students would not be forced to read lips. Their efforts, along with her interactions with other individuals with impaired hearing, moved Deegii. As a result, her youth empowerment project began to include sign language interpreters for events and presentations.

This work influenced Deegii. She and her friends wrote a guidebook about how to accomplish your dreams and obtain a scholarship. Her marketing talk turned into an empowerment speech. "I found so much joy and fulfillment in speaking to young people," she says. "It felt right. I spoke not out of a script, but really out of a beating heart."

Yet Deegii wanted to do work that had more direct impact, one that helped save lives. By this time, she was a single mother. She moved back to Minnesota with her children to pursue a master's degree in human rights at the University of Minnesota. The focus for her degree was on civilian protection in conflict-affected areas. She is not sure where her journey will take her next, but she looks forward to discovering new opportunities.

For the Mongolian lunar new year, family and friends gather to celebrate. They greet each other formally, in a way that respects the elders and invites others to share their joy at overcoming the harsh and heavy winter. For a traditionally nomadic people, the end of winter and the coming of spring signal safety and reunion. This holiday also serves as a time for reconciliation and unity between family and friends. Like many Mongolians, Deegii often serves *buuz* (pronounced "booze"), steamed dumplings filled with meat, vegetables, and spices. She often serves it with potato salad, in a cultural fusion of Mongolian and Russian influence that goes beyond the familiar American picnic variation.

Buuz (Mongolian Dumplings)

Makes 45 or more dumplings

DOUGH

1 tablespoon salt

5 cups flour, plus extra for rolling dough

FILLING

1 pound raw ground lamb

1 green bell pepper, stemmed, seeded, and diced

½ onion, finely diced

4 garlic cloves, peeled and minced

10 stems flat-leaf parsley, finely chopped (both stems and leaves)

1 cup chopped kale, stems removed

1 handful fresh spinach, chopped (about 1 cup)

1½ tablespoons soy sauce

½ teaspoon salt

¼ teaspoon freshly ground black pepper

TO MAKE THE DOUGH: Put 1 tablespoon salt in a large bowl with 2 cups plus 2 tablespoons warm water, and stir to dissolve. Add the flour, and mix with your hands until combined. Knead the dough in the bowl for 5 to 10 minutes, adding a bit more flour if needed, to make a stiff, dry dough. Place the dough on a lightly floured work surface and cover it with the bowl to rest for about 30 minutes while you make the filling.

TO MAKE THE FILLING: In a large bowl, combine the lamb, bell pepper, onion, garlic, parsley, kale, spinach, soy sauce, ½ teaspoon salt, black pepper, and ⅓ cup water. Mix all the ingredients together well.

TO ASSEMBLE THE DUMPLINGS: Knead the dough on a lightly floured work surface for about 5 minutes. Break off a chunk about the size of a fist (4 to 5 inches in diameter) and roll it into a log 1 to 2 inches in diameter. Cut the log into 1-inch pieces. Place a small amount of flour in a bowl. With your hands, roll each piece into a ball, then toss the balls in the flour to lightly cover them.

Lightly flour your work surface. Working quickly, use a rolling pin to flatten each ball into a disk about ¼ inch thick and 2 to 3 inches in diameter. Hold the disk in one hand and place 1 to 2 teaspoons of filling at the center of the disk. Create an oval dumpling by pinching the dough together at one end of the disk, then bringing the edges up, pinching them lightly together to enclose the filling. You can plait or fold the edges as you go for a decorative look (see photograph).

Place a steamer basket in a pot with gently boiling water. Place a single layer of dumplings in the basket (do not let the water touch the dumplings). Cover and steam for 20 to 22 minutes. Carefully remove the lid, preventing any water from falling back onto the dumplings. Transfer the steamed dumplings to a plate. Repeat to steam the remaining dumplings. Serve with ketchup (yes, ketchup

is a condiment in Mongolia). Uncooked dumplings can be frozen individually on a baking sheet, and then kept in a freezer bag or container in the freezer. To cook later, remove them from the freezer and immediately steam them for 25 minutes.

Russian–Mongolian Potato Salad

Serves 6 to 8

NOTE: Plan ahead to hard-cook the eggs in advance. Deegii uses canned peas in the salad.

3 to 4 eggs

5 large Russet potatoes, peeled and cut into small cubes (about 4 heaping cups)

1 large carrot, peeled and cut into cubes

4 smoked sausages, cut into cubes

¼ white onion, finely chopped

About ½ cup diced dill pickles, patted dry, reserving 1 teaspoon of pickle juice, optional

About ½ cup green peas (see Note)

1 cup mayonnaise, plus up to ½ cup more, as desired

1 teaspoon salt

½ teaspoon freshly ground black pepper

TO MAKE HARD-COOKED EGGS: Place the eggs in a small pan, cover with water, and bring to a boil over medium-high heat. Remove the pan from the heat, cover the pan, and let sit for 15 minutes. Drain the water and add cold water, repeating until the eggs have cooled. Refrigerate until ready to use.

TO PREPARE THE SALAD: Place the potatoes and carrots in a large pot over high heat and cover with water by a few inches. Bring to a boil and cook until the potatoes and carrots are just tender but still firm, about 12 minutes. Drain in a colander and let the potatoes and carrots cool to room temperature.

In a skillet over medium-high heat, fry the sausages until browned. Transfer them to a plate lined with paper towels and allow the sausages to cool to room temperature.

In a large bowl, combine the potatoes, carrots, sausages, onion, pickles and reserved pickle juice (optional), peas, mayonnaise, salt, and black pepper. Mix carefully. Peel and chop the eggs. Fold them gently into the salad. Refrigerate until ready to serve, but allow the salad to warm up to near room temperature before serving.

Russian-Mongolian
Potato Salad

OLGA BARANOVA

RUSSIA

Olga Baranova is a passionate human rights and LGBTQIA+ activist. She is also a mother. As founder of the Moscow Community Center for LGBT+ Initiatives (MCC), she accepted the personal risks inherent in her work in Russia, but when that activity put her son at risk, she and her wife knew they had to leave.

Olga was born near Moscow and earned an engineering degree in Ukraine, after which she moved to Moscow. But as the city was hostile to the LGBTQIA+ community, she felt she needed to conceal her sexual orientation to avoid discrimination. When Olga and her girlfriend, now wife, decided to have a child, they moved to Sweden where they knew they would be accepted. She and her family later returned to Moscow seeking the same acceptance but found that nothing had changed.

In response, she embraced activism and, in 2015, founded the MCC, building a platform for recognition, resources, and legal support for the LGBTQIA+ community in Russia. MCC has received international acclaim for its lifesaving work, in particular evacuating LGBTQIA+ youth from Chechnya due to the escalation in violence targeting people on the basis of their sexual orientation and gender identity/expression. That work is documented in the Oscar-nominated HBO documentary *Welcome to Chechnya* (www.welcometochechnya.com).

Olga's work made remaining in Russia increasingly dangerous. She was visible and her actions well-known. Family members of youth she helped evacuate were tracking her down. So, Olga moved her son out of the country to Ukraine, where he lived temporarily with her mother. Once he reached school age, Olga brought him back to Russia. Given the general hostility toward LBGTQIA+ people in Russia, particularly parents in same-sex relationships, Olga's greatest fear was that she would go to school to pick him up one day and he would be gone. It was time to leave.

Her wife and son went to the United States first. Olga followed, coming to Minneapolis as part of a collaborative project between MCC and the Advocates for Human Rights. She made the decision that she could not return to Russia, given it wasn't safe for her son and that she needed to be with him and her wife, and they applied for asylum.

Initially Olga didn't realize how difficult it would be to change countries. The United States was not Russia, and her life had just been "turned on its head," as she described it. Being a tourist was not the same as trying to create a home for her family. Everything was different, and every day there was something new that required adjustment: housing, bank systems, transportation, taxes. Her life lost its order and stress crept in.

But after five years, Olga has found her routine in the United States. Her activism continues, working remotely for MCC, which has partnered with the Advocates since 2016.

Though the United States is now home, she has not forgotten Moscow. Olga fondly remembers the days when she stayed home to raise her son when he was small. She cooked for her family and shares a recipe that is one of her son's favorites. It is simple to prepare, flexible with ingredients, and can serve a family or easily be expanded to feed a larger group.

Olga Baranova

Sheet-pan Chicken and Potatoes

Serves 4

- 2 onions, sliced about ⅛ to ¼ inch thick
- 4 potatoes, unpeeled and cut into slices or quarters
- Olive oil
- Salt and freshly ground pepper, to taste
- 4 boneless chicken breasts
- 3 to 3½ teaspoons prepared Italian spice mix seasoning
- 4 garlic cloves, cut in slivers, or more garlic, to taste
- ¼ to ⅔ cup Parmesan cheese, optional

NOTE: For a variation, after cooking is complete, add 1 to 2 tablespoons capers to the chicken and potatoes, and squeeze half a lemon over the dish before serving. Cut the remaining lemon into slices or wedges and serve with the meal.

Preheat the oven to 425°F and line a half-sheet pan with aluminum foil, with enough extra foil to cover the ingredients.

Arrange the onions on the foil as the first layer. In a bowl, drizzle the potatoes with a little olive oil and toss to coat. Add salt and pepper to taste, as well as any mix of herbs or spices (Olga uses an Italian spice mix). Toss the potatoes with the herbs and spread over the onions to make a second layer.

Cut slits in the chicken breasts and place slivers of garlic in each. Place the chicken breasts on top of the potatoes. Close the foil over the ingredients and place the sheet pan in the oven. Bake until the potatoes are tender, about 25 minutes. Open the foil and leave it open for about 5 minutes to release the steam. Then sprinkle Parmesan cheese on top (optional).

Serve with a salad of lettuce, tomatoes, cucumbers, fresh basil, green onions, cheese, salt, and olive oil. Also serve with a dry white wine or vodka and a side of pickles.

Sheet-pan Chicken and Potatoes

VERÓNICA CADAVID GONZÁLEZ

COLOMBIA

Cooking can inspire many surprises, including discussions of human rights. Verónica Cadavid González, a human rights advocate from a family of Colombian coffee farmers, found that to be the case during a workshop in her country that focused on discussing armed conflict and violence among people who had been displaced. While such serious moments generally take place in a formal setting, this gathering was held in a kitchen as the participants measured ingredients, stirred pots, and told stories as they cooked.

On another occasion, Verónica worked with a memory project that used a cooking lab to commemorate and celebrate the Afro-Colombian culture of her homeland, where violence had displaced many communities from traditional lands (more than eight million people are internally displaced in Colombia). That's the power behind memory, stories, and cooking.

Verónica has worked in human rights since she began law school in 2013 in Colombia. By 2020, she attended the University of Minnesota to earn a master's degree in human rights. Her work is shaped by the principle of empowering those who seek protection. She wants to hear their views as advocates so they can help shape better policies. This makes them not only beneficiaries, but also actors in their own advocacy. Verónica was influenced by her work collecting testimonies of those who had experienced violence for the House of Memory Museum, Museo Casa de la Memoria, in her home city of Medellín, Colombia. Making those voices heard was the central purpose behind the museum, fostering collective memory as reparation and as a way for victims to heal.

"It was an opportunity at the museum to get out from my comfort zone because I was a human rights lawyer very much on the legal side, and this was a huge multidisciplinary project," she says. That dedication and passion has driven her to work with international justice, including a stint at the United Nations.

And her love of cooking travels with her. "It's the way that I get out my stress," says Verónica. "I can go home and cook for lunch." She's also found that meals are a useful way to interact with others while doing legal work, without wearing her lawyer hat. She lives near her office at the Advocates of Human Rights, where she deals with the issues of international justice and women's rights.

Bandeja paisa is the signature dish in Antioquía, in the Andes mountains, where her family still lives. The name of the dish describes both the food and the whole identity of the people (*paisas*) who live in the region. It's a huge plate piled with beans and *chicharrón* (fried pork belly), plantains and rice, and Colombian sausage. "Add avocado and more, and you need a four-hour nap after this," she says.

"The dish was done centuries ago when people were doing all this hard labor, like farming, and they needed to be very well-fed. I love to make this. But you need a big group of people to serve it to."

Verónica Cadavid González

Bandeja Paisa (Colombian Meat Platter)

Serves 6 to 8

This is a feast for the eyes—as well as the stomach—and definitely for a crowd.

NOTE: Plan ahead, as the *cargamanto* beans (also called cranberry beans, which originated in Colombia) must be soaked overnight. To prepare parts of this meal ahead, make the *Hogao* first, as it is used in the *Frijoles Antioqueños*. Don't be daunted by the many steps, which are very basic.

FOR THE PLATTER

Cooked white rice, enough for all

Fried plantains (recipe on page 55)

3 to 4 avocados (½ avocado per person), diced or sliced (but do this last so the avocado doesn't brown)

Hogao

Arepas de maiz (corn *arepas*), heated in the oven (can be found frozen in Colombian stores)

Frijoles Antioqueños

Chicharrón

Powdered Beef

Colombian Chorizo

TO ASSEMBLE THE PLATTER OF *BANDEJA PAISA*: Place the beans at the center of the serving plate and surround with separate piles of rice, plantains, avocado, *chicharrón*, powdered beef, and sausage, if using. Serve with *arepas de maiz*. Put any extra Hogao in a bowl on the platter.

(recipes continue on page 114)

Bandeja Paisa

HOGAO

Makes about 1½ cups

This tomato–onion mixture is traditional with Bandeja Paisa.

- 2 teaspoons sunflower oil or other neutral oil
- 1½ cups finely chopped onion (all white onion, or a mixture of white onion and green onions)
- 2 cups finely chopped tomatoes (2 to 4 very ripe)
- 1 garlic clove, chopped
- ½ teaspoon salt
- ¼ teaspoon ground cumin, optional

Combine the oil, onion, tomatoes, garlic, salt, and cumin in a saucepan over medium heat. Cook, stirring occasionally, for about 15 minutes. Tomatoes should have broken down and softened quite a bit when done. Use *Hogao* with the beans, and add any remainder to serve on the platter.

FRIJOLES ANTIOQUEÑOS (COLOMBIAN BEANS)

Makes 7 to 8 cups

- 1 pound dry red beans (*cargamanto* or cranberry beans, or other small red beans such as pinto or kidney), covered generously with water and soaked overnight
- 2 carrots, each cut in half
- 1 green plantain, chopped into small cubes
- ½ onion, peeled and stemmed
- 1 garlic clove, peeled
- 1 slice uncooked bacon, optional
- ¼ teaspoon ground cumin, optional
- 1 cup *Hogao*, divided (see recipe above)
- About 1 tablespoon ketchup
- Salt

NOTE: Plan ahead to soak the beans overnight.

Drain the water from the beans and place them in a pressure cooker or a standard pot with the carrots, plantain, onion, garlic, bacon (optional), and cumin (optional). Add eight cups new water. Bring to a boil, then reduce to a simmer and cook until the beans are tender and starting to pop open, about 40 minutes in a pressure cooker or about 60 to 70 minutes in a pot over medium-low heat. If using a standard pot for the beans, check and stir occasionally, adding more water as needed.

Place the carrots, onion, garlic, and about 1 cup of the beans and water in a blender. Blend with ½ cup of the *Hogao* until smooth and add the mixture back to the pot. Stir in the remaining ½ cup *Hogao* and the ketchup and salt. Cook on low heat for 20 to 30 more minutes, stirring occasionally until the beans are soft and the broth has thickened a bit.

COLOMBIAN *CHICHARRÓN* (FRIED PORK BELLY)

3 to 4 pounds Colombian *chicharrón* (pork belly)

Salt, to taste

1 teaspoon baking soda

About 3 tablespoons vegetable oil

NOTE: Colombian *chicharrón* is a special cut and available at Mexican or Latin American stores.

Make small cuts with a knife in the fatty side of the *chicharrón*. Sprinkle both sides with salt. Sprinkle the baking soda on the fatty side and rub it in.

Fry the *chicharrón* in oil over low heat, uncovered, for about 15 to 20 minutes, until it is brown and crispy. Flip once or twice during cooking. Alternatively, cook it in an air fryer at 350°F for about 20 minutes.

POWDERED BEEF

½ pound flank or hangar steak, sliced thin (about 6 slices, ¼ inch thick)

Salt

2 tablespoons cooking oil

Sprinkle the steak with salt on both sides and fry in oil over medium heat until brown and completely cooked through. Set aside to cool completely. Then cut into small pieces and use a food processor to grind the meat into a powder. If you do not have a food processor, finely mince the meat.

COLOMBIAN CHORIZO

This is another extra for the platter, if desired.

½ chorizo sausage per person

Vegetable oil

In a skillet, fry the sausages over medium-high heat in a bit of oil until browned and cooked through.

STEPHANIE WILLMAN BORDAT

MOROCCO

Immigration is a two-way street: People immigrate to the United States from other countries for many reasons; American citizens also emigrate *from* the United States to other countries. That was the case for Stephanie Willman Bordat, international human rights activist and cofounder of Mobilising for Rights Associates. She was born in the United States but has called Morocco home for more than two decades.

Stephanie's family moved frequently when she was a child—Maine, Mississippi, Colorado, New York City. She learned early that wherever they went, it meant something different to be a girl. At each location, she was confronted with new norms and conflicting messages. When Stephanie enrolled at Swarthmore College near Philadelphia, she began to look at women's rights, which led to volunteering at women's nonprofits. Then,

Stephanie Willman Bordat

by chance, she was introduced to Morocco. Stephanie registered for a sociology class on gender roles and was assigned to read a book by Minnesota author Susan Schaefer Davis. *Patience and Power: Women's Lives in a Moroccan Village* was an eye-opening read on women's power. Stephanie immediately knew what she wanted to do with her life. She saw similarities between Morocco and her experience growing up in the United States, where both countries were at crossroads that included contradictory views of women. Stephanie felt she could make an impact.

She single-mindedly pursued her work with women's rights and her move to Morocco. She was awarded a Fulbright grant and went to Morocco to study, intending to stay for one year, but extended it to four. In the process, she understood she would not be content to be an observer of the changes going on in the world. Rather, she chose to be an advocate for change. Her next step was to leave Morocco to attend a joint law school program, where she divided her time between Columbia Law School in New York City and the Sorbonne in Paris. The latter was critical because the legal system in Morocco is based on French law.

After obtaining her dual degree, Stephanie felt obligated to use the skills and capabilities she had honed in law school. Her goal was always to focus on women's rights activism, but she wanted to use her skills somewhere she felt she could be of service to others. There were plenty of lawyers equipped to do this work in the United States, but Morocco was in a dynamic region with the potential for major changes in women's rights and family law. Stephanie wanted to be part of it.

Through some luck and considerable perseverance, Stephanie met and began working with Saida Kouzzi, who became a business partner. They eventually co-founded MRA (which means "woman" in Arabic), an international nonprofit organization based in Rabat, Morocco, that works across northwest Africa. MRA's mission is to promote women's human rights. It uses a grassroots approach to foster voice and empowerment to people who have been historically excluded.

What is home to Stephanie? "It depends on my mood at the moment," she says jokingly. After growing up in the United States and living for so long in Morocco, with two children born there and a French husband, she has ties to three countries. All offer her a sense of home.

MRA has been a long-time partner with the Advocates for Human Rights, conducting training and workshops together on issues of discrimination and violence against women since 2007. MRA also works with local nongovernmental organizations (NGOs), some of which provide programs that teach skills, such as cooking, that provide women with the ability to earn an income. The recipes come from two of these NGOs: Chicken *Pastilla* from the Association Amal for Women and Development in El Hajeb, Morocco, and Chicken Couscous with Vegetables from the Association Tafiil Moubadarat in Taza, Morocco.

Bessah we Raha! To your health!

Chicken *Pastilla* (Moroccan Chicken Pie)

Serves 8

NOTE: Plan ahead, as the frozen phyllo sheets need to be thawed according to package directions before use. The large amount of oil that goes in the recipe is correct. You will need a pastry brush.

- 3 pounds boneless, skinless chicken thighs, rubbed with lemon and salt
- 2 onions, chopped
- 1 bunch fresh flat-leaf parsley, left intact
- 4 or 5 cinnamon sticks
- A few strands of saffron infused in 1 cup water
- 2 teaspoons ground ginger
- 1 teaspoon freshly ground black pepper
- Salt, to taste
- 2 teaspoons ground turmeric
- ⅔ cup olive oil (or mixture of vegetable oil and olive oil), plus more for the almonds
- 1 tablespoon honey
- 6 eggs
- 2 cups silvered almonds
- 1 tablespoon powdered sugar, plus more for decoration
- 1 tablespoon ground cinnamon, plus more for decoration
- 1 (1-pound) box phyllo sheets, thawed according to package directions
- ½ cup (1 stick) butter or more, melted

TO PREPARE THE FILLING: Preheat the oven to 350°F. Put the chicken pieces, onions, parsley, cinnamon sticks, saffron with the water, ginger, black pepper, salt, turmeric, and ⅔ cup olive oil (or mixture of vegetable oil and olive oil) in a large pot over low heat and cook until the chicken is done. Remove the chicken from the pot and set it aside. Discard the cinnamon sticks and parsley.

Add the honey to the pot and continue to stir. Whisk the eggs and add them a little at a time to the pot, while stirring constantly, until all is well-combined and the eggs are set. Transfer the onion and egg mixture to a colander to drain it of any remaining oil.

Cut the chicken into very small pieces. Sauté the almonds in a little oil, then chop them finely and sprinkle with about 1 tablespoon powdered sugar and 1 tablespoon cinnamon.

TO ASSEMBLE: Unwrap the phyllo sheets. You will be using all of them. Cover the phyllo with a damp cloth while you are working on the assembly, so it doesn't dry out, removing sheets only as you need them. Use a pastry brush to brush melted butter on the sides and bottom of a 9- or 10-inch round springform pan or other baking dish. Brush melted butter on each of a few phyllo sheets at a time, layering the sheets one by one. You will need to work your way around the round pan with the phyllo sheets to cover the whole area (or use a 9- by 13-inch pan, if preferred). Either set a few phyllo sheets aside to cover the top or plan to use the phyllo overhanging the edge of the pan to fold over the top (like in a rustic tart). Add the onion and egg mixture, almonds, and chicken in layers until the filling is used up. Finish with a layer of almonds, setting some aside to decorate the finished dish.

Either fold over the phyllo overhang (as noted earlier) or put a final sheet of phyllo over the mixture to cover; then tuck underneath to

Chicken *Pastilla*

close. Brush melted butter on the top of the last sheet of phyllo that serves as the cover. Bake until nicely browned, about 20 to 30 minutes.

TO SERVE: Decorate the top with almonds, powdered sugar, and cinnamon.

Chicken Couscous with Vegetables

Serves 6

NOTE: Plan ahead, as the chickpeas (also known as garbanzo beans) must be soaked overnight. In Morocco, couscous is traditionally steamed over a pot of simmering water or broth using a *couscoussier*, or couscous maker (available online). This yields a lighter and fluffier version of couscous. If a couscous maker is not available, couscous can be made with a steamer (such as that used for vegetables), which is how the recipe was tested. The chicken and vegetables were cooked separately from the couscous. The original recipe was designed for a large gathering but has been halved to accommodate a smaller meal. *Smen* is a salted, fermented butter used in Morocco and other North African cuisine. It can be purchased in specialty grocery stores or online.

CHICKEN

¾ cup dry chickpeas, soaked overnight (see Note)
1¾ pounds chicken, cut in pieces
1 onion, chopped
1 tomato, puréed
½ cup olive oil or neutral vegetable oil
1½ teaspoons freshly grated black pepper
1 tablespoon ground ginger

TO MAKE THE CHICKEN AND VEGETABLES: Drain the chickpeas. In a large stock pot over medium heat, combine the chicken, chopped onions, tomato, chickpeas, ½ cup oil, 1½ teaspoons black pepper, 1 tablespoon ginger, ½ tablespoon salt, ½ teaspoon saffron with water, 1½ teaspoons turmeric, cinnamon sticks, cilantro, and parsley and cook until the chicken is browned on both sides, about 15 minutes.

Add boiling water to cover the chicken and simmer for 20 minutes.

Add the carrots and cabbage and cook for 15 minutes more. Add the turnips, hot pepper, squash, and zucchini and cook until the chicken and vegetables are tender, about 15 minutes. Remove the pot from the heat and transfer the chicken to a plate and cover. Transfer the vegetables and broth to a large bowl.

TO MAKE THE COUSCOUS: If the holes of your steamer are larger than the couscous grains, use a coffee filter or cheesecloth on the bottom to keep the couscous from falling through. You will be steaming the couscous three times.

In a large bowl, combine the couscous, ½ teaspoon salt, and 1 tablespoon oil, and mix well with your hands until all the couscous grains are well-coated. Add 1 cup cold water, letting the couscous absorb all the water. Toss and rub lightly to remove any clumps. Bring water in the bottom of the steamer to a gentle boil over medium heat. Place the couscous in the steamer, cover, and steam for 15 minutes.

Remove the steamer from the heat. Transfer the couscous to the bowl, add 1 cup cold water, and let the couscous absorb it. Toss the couscous and rub lightly. Transfer the couscous back to the steamer, cover and steam for 15 minutes.

½ tablespoon salt

½ teaspoon crushed saffron added to 1 tablespoon water

1½ teaspoons ground turmeric

1 to 2 cinnamon sticks, to taste

½ bunch fresh cilantro (a large handful), stems removed

½ bunch flat-leaf parsley (a large handful), stems removed

½ pound carrots, peeled and halved lengthwise

½ pound (small) cabbage, cut into 4 pieces

½ pound white turnips, peeled and halved

1 hot pepper (such as jalapeño), or to taste, seeded and chopped

½ pound (about 1 cup) butternut or acorn squash, cut in large pieces

½ pound zucchini, ends removed, sliced lengthwise into several pieces

COUSCOUS

1 pound medium couscous

½ teaspoon salt

1 tablespoon olive or neutral vegetable oil

1½ teaspoons Moroccan preserved butter (*smen*; see Note), optional

CARAMELIZED ONIONS (*TFAIA*)

1 pound onions, thinly sliced

½ teaspoon saffron, crushed and added to 1 tablespoon water

½ teaspoon freshly ground black pepper

1 teaspoon ground ginger

½ teaspoon salt

¼ cup olive or neutral vegetable oil

¾ cup raisins

¼ cup superfine sugar

1½ teaspoons ground cinnamon

Remove the steamer from the heat. Transfer the couscous to the bowl, add 1 cup of cold water, and let the couscous absorb it. Toss the couscous and rub lightly. Transfer the couscous back to the steamer, cover and steam for 15 minutes.

Remove the steamer from the heat. Transfer the couscous to the bowl and add the *smen*, if using. Mix well, cover, and set aside until the final presentation.

TO MAKE THE CARAMELIZED ONIONS (*TFAIA*): In a skillet over low heat, combine the sliced onions, ½ teaspoon saffron with water, ½ teaspoon black pepper, 1 teaspoon ginger, ½ teaspoon salt, and ¼ cup oil. Cook the onions until they become transparent.

Add the raisins, ½ cup water, sugar, and 1½ teaspoons ground cinnamon. Mix well and cook on low heat until the onions caramelize.

TO ASSEMBLE: Spread the couscous on a large platter. Hollow out the middle and fill it with the chicken. Separate the vegetables and place them individually in a spoke-like manner from the chicken to the edge of the platter. Scatter the chickpeas around the vegetables. Place the caramelized onions in a separate bowl on the side, for serving.

Drizzle the couscous and vegetables with a little of the broth from the chicken and place the rest of the broth in a bowl to serve with the meal.

couscous

KITCHENS OF HOPE

Hope keeps us moving forward as we look for fresh possibilities. Bridget Chivimbiso Chigunwe fled Zimbabwe to avoid persecution and today studies to be a nurse. As a child, Loan Huynh and her family escaped the fall of Saigon, and she now works as an immigration lawyer. Halima Mohamed of Somalia spent years in a refugee camp before starting a food business that helps her fellow Somalians in the Twin Cities. Haydee, a lawyer in El Salvador, left her country after her job became too dangerous. Today, Yia Vang, who was born in a refugee camp in Thailand, is a chef who reflects his Hmong heritage. What they all have in common is hope for a new life, forged in part in the kitchen.

BRIDGET CHIVIMBISO CHIGUNWE

ZIMBABWE

Bridget Chivimbiso Chigunwe's life began in the small farming town of Norton in Zimbabwe, where everybody knew one another. She grew up in a large family, with her father who was a teacher and then a school principal. "Education was very expensive, but food was cheap," says Bridget about Zimbabwe. People grew their own food or would share the fresh produce, meat, and poultry they had. "In Zimbabwe, you don't charge; you give," says Bridget. People gathered to celebrate many special occasions, and no invitation was needed. Everyone was welcome for the festivities. "And we dance," Bridget says. "We dance a lot."

Yet she also became a police target, and in 2015 she fled the country to escape persecution. Leaving by way of Botswana and South Africa, Bridget later landed in Panama, then traveled north through Costa Rica, Nicaragua, Honduras, Guatemala, and Mexico. She walked almost that entire journey, with bus rides as occasional respites. In Central America and Mexico, the foods and culture were similar to those from home. Bridget found many farmers eating produce from their garden.

Bridget Chivimbiso Chigunwe

"The people were very welcoming," she says. "They will even call you over to eat. 'Come and eat, come and eat. Are you short of money for the bus?'"

At the U.S. entry point where she was interviewed, an immigration official gave Bridget a pass, a bus ticket, and $50. She still remembers the official's name. In September 2016, Bridget was released in California, traveling next to North Dakota before settling in Minnesota, where she came to the Community-University Health Care Center in Minneapolis. She found a home at Missionaries for Charity, which referred her to the Advocates for Human Rights. This led her to a lawyer who assisted her with a petition for asylum, which took six years to be heard. For much of that time, she served as a certified nursing assistant and health care technician, providing care to people throughout the pandemic. Bridget also attended college, where she is on track to earn her nursing degree. She finally received asylum in 2022, and at last can let go of her fears. She now serves on the board of directors for the Advocates.

"I love Minnesota," says Bridget, who buys fresh produce at the farmers market. She loves to cook and uses fresh food whenever possible. Bridget's recipe is for a spicy stewed beef served with kale and *Sadza*, a traditional porridge from her country.

Nyama Ine Muto

Nyama Ine Muto (Beef Stew)

Makes 3 cups (serves 4)

4 tablespoons vegetable oil, divided

1½ teaspoons salt

1 pound stew beef, cut into bite-sized pieces

1 sweet onion, diced

1 teaspoon garlic powder or 1 garlic clove, diced

2 tablespoons roughly chopped fresh dill, or 1 tablespoon dried

1 teaspoon freshly ground black pepper

1 teaspoon red pepper flakes, optional

2½ large tomatoes, coarsely cut, or ½ (15-ounce) can crushed tomatoes

2 tablespoons tomato paste, optional

Put 2 tablespoons vegetable oil in a deep, medium-sized stew pot. Add the salt and 1½ cups cold water. Put the meat in the salted water, and boil uncovered until the water evaporates, about 35 to 40 minutes. When the beef has about 10 more minutes to boil, begin to make the *Sadza* (see recipe, page 127).

When all the water in the pot is gone, add 2 tablespoons more oil and fry the meat for about 5 minutes. Add the onion and garlic and cook until the onions are translucent. Add the dill, black pepper, and red pepper flakes (optional) and stir to coat everything. Add the tomatoes and mix while crushing chunky pieces. Mix until smooth. Add a little water for a thinner stew or add a tablespoon or two of the tomato paste for a thicker version. Let simmer for 5 minutes. Adjust salt, if needed. Serve with *Sadza* and kale.

fresh dill

Muriwo Wemubindu (Sautéed Kale)

Serves 4

- 2 tablespoons vegetable oil
- 2 bundles of kale, stemmed, rinsed, and thinly chopped (about 6 cups)
- ½ teaspoon salt
- ¼ teaspoon pepper, optional

NOTE: Lacinato (dinosaur kale) works well with this dish. If using a curly kale variety, blanch the stemmed leaves in a large pot of boiling water for a few minutes before chopping.

Put the oil in a medium-sized skillet over medium heat. Add the kale and sauté for 5 minutes. Sprinkle with salt and pepper (optional) and serve.

Sadza (Porridge)

Serves 4

- 1 cup plus 1 to 2 tablespoons finely ground corn flour (such as Indian Head or masa harina), or farina flour, divided

Bring 3 cups water to a boil in a medium-sized pot. In the meantime, in a small bowl, use a fork to stir together 1 cup cold water and 1 cup corn or farina flour until well combined.

When the water boils, carefully add the flour mixture, stirring vigorously with a spoon. Bring the mixture to a boil again, stirring frequently, then lower heat and simmer, covered, for 10 to 15 minutes, stirring occasionally. When the mixture is thick and smooth, add 1 to 2 tablespoons more corn or farina flour, if needed for the desired texture. *Sadza* should not be watery or too dense. Cover the pot again and keep over low heat for another 3 to 5 minutes. Serve with the beef stew and kale.

LOAN HUYNH

VIETNAM

Loan Huynh fled Vietnam with her family in 1975, racing along the beach the night Saigon fell, in a Jeep chased by exploding shells. They were rescued by a ship captain, who brought them to safety. When they arrived in a refugee camp in Fort Chaffee, Arkansas, Loan was five years old. The United States offered both challenge and promise. She recalls her excitement holding a scroll of the Declaration of Independence, handed out during an elementary school Bicentennial celebration. Yet as she and her sister walked home that day, schoolmates attacked them—their first experience of anti-immigrant sentiment and racism.

Life in the United States was not always easy. Loan's parents worked twelve-hour days at their small grocery in the Fifth Ward in Houston, Texas. Her father lost his eye in an attack at the grocery store that forever changed his life. Despite the hardships and the sense of being caught between two worlds, the humanity that Loan witnessed and the remembrance of the power of one to make a difference formed the basis of her passion for human rights.

Loan earned her law degree and moved to Minnesota for a staff position as an attorney with the Advocates for Human Rights in 1996, where she represented those seeking

Loan Huynh and her mother

asylum and struggling to adapt to a new culture. This move was the first time she had left her parents' home, and the Advocates soon became her family. She now chairs the immigration department at Fredrikson & Byron law firm but remains a volunteer at the Advocates.

A proud moment for her at the Advocates was an event called Celebrating with Community that was planned by the refugee and immigrant program team. Clients were recognized and the food of their countries were served, donated from immigrant-owned restaurants.

"We knew that no matter how far our asylum clients were from their home countries, they could find home in the foods they brought with them to the United States," Loan says. She has found, through decades of talking with people, "that food offers a segue into their lives and experiences," she says. "It opens people up."

That was how her mother raised and loved her children. "Cooking and food is her language of love for her five children and now her grandbabies," Loan says. "No matter how little we had, feeding her children was about hope and survival." For her mother, no matter how many hours a day she worked, the dinner table was filled with Vietnamese dishes. "These dishes embodied her love for us, the memories of her life in Vietnam, her own mom and seven siblings that she left in Vietnam, and a part of her soul," Loan says. "As long as she could feed her children, her dreams and hope for us remained alive."

Pho (pronounced "FUH") defines Vietnam like no other dish. "It's not difficult to make if you know the steps," says Loan about the soup that is prepared in layers, with beef bones cooked for hours to make a clear golden broth, with charred ginger and whole onions, and spices that all add the complex flavors. "*Pho is* my mom," Loan says. "*Pho* is the one dish that my mom makes for you that brings you straight home. It's the heart and soul for many families." Yet everyone has their own version. "We think our mom's version is the best, of course," says Loan.

Many Vietnamese cooks add fish sauce to the broth while simmering. "However, our mother found that it can add a slight sourness to the finished broth so, in our family, we add the fish sauce to the bowl of *pho* just before serving," says Loan. Her mother recommends Three Crabs Fish Sauce, but many brands are available.

Even though this is called Vietnamese Beef *Pho*, the recipe includes whole chicken and chicken broth (either homemade or canned will work). Without the fresh chicken and canned broth, the *pho* lacks depth and dimension, Loan says.

Vietnamese Beef *Pho*

Vietnamese Beef *Pho* (Beef Soup with Noodles)

Makes 8 large servings

NOTE: Plan ahead, as the broth needs to simmer for 8 hours. This recipe uses a lot of meat. Rock sugar can be found at Asian stores, as can *bò viên* meatballs, which are frozen and already cooked. *Culantro* (*ngo gai*) has a similar flavor to cilantro and can be found at Vietnamese or Asian markets.

BROTH

- 3 pounds beef bones (a mix of oxtails cut into 2-inch pieces and shank bones preferred)
- 1 whole chicken, cut in pieces
- 1 to 2 pounds of beef brisket or boneless short ribs
- 6 (16-ounce) cans (or 96 ounces) chicken broth, divided
- 1 cinnamon stick
- 2 star anise pods
- 1 whole nutmeg, optional
- 1 large piece of ginger root, about 3½ to 4½ inches, unpeeled
- 1 large yellow onion, peeled
- 3 to 4 pieces of rock sugar (see Note)
- Kosher salt, to taste

star anise pods

TO PREPARE THE BONES: Put the beef bones in a large stockpot with enough water to cover them. Bring the water to a boil, and boil for about 4 minutes, until the film rises to the top. Drain the bones in a large strainer and rinse with cold water; set aside. This step will create a clean, clear broth for the *pho*.

Cut the chicken breast meat off the bones. Set the chicken breasts aside to poach later in the *pho* broth. Preheat the oven to broil (500°F).

TO PREPARE THE BROTH: Return the beef bones to the large stockpot, along with the chicken bones, and the brisket (or short ribs). Add enough cold water to fill about half of the pot. Add 80 ounces (5 cans) of the chicken broth. Bring to a boil over high heat.

While the stock is heating up, place the cinnamon, star anise, nutmeg (optional), ginger root, and whole onion on a baking sheet. Broil in the oven just until fragrant and lightly golden brown. The star anise will brown quickly; remove it after about 20 to 30 seconds. The cinnamon and nutmeg will brown after about 2 minutes. Do not burn the spices, or you'll have to start over. Remove the ginger root and onions when edges are charred.

Transfer the cinnamon, anise, and nutmeg to the stockpot (wrapped in cheesecloth, if you prefer). Allow the ginger root to cool, then slice it lengthwise. Add the ginger root and onion to the stockpot along with 3 pieces of rock sugar and about 2 heaping tablespoons of kosher salt. Bring to a boil, then reduce heat to a low simmer. Remove the film as it rises to the surface while the broth is simmering. Avoid stirring the broth as much as possible while the broth simmers for about 8 hours.

(recipe and ingredients continue on page 132)

PHO

- 1 package of *bò viên* beef meatballs, optional (see Note)
- 3 (16-ounce) packages of fresh rice noodles
- 1 pound eye-of-round beef, thinly sliced
- 1 small white onion, thinly sliced
- 1 cup chopped green onions
- 1 cup freshly chopped cilantro
- Freshly ground black pepper
- Fish sauce (see Note)
- 2 cups fresh bean sprouts
- 2 handfuls Thai basil sprigs
- 2 handfuls fresh *culantro* (*ngo gai*; see Note)
- 6 Thai bird's eye chiles, whole, or 1 jalapeño chile, thinly sliced
- 2 limes, cut into wedges
- Pickled onions, optional
- Sriracha sauce, optional
- Hoisin sauce, optional

Remove the brisket (or short ribs) when tender, after 3 to 4 hours. Allow the brisket (or short ribs) to cool completely in the refrigerator before thinly slicing it for later.

Add the chicken breasts to the stockpot. When the chicken breasts are cooked through, remove them from the broth, and allow them to cool. When cool, slice the chicken into ¼-inch slices. Arrange them on a plate, cover, and place in the refrigerator until ready to use.

After the broth has simmered for about 6 hours, top it off with the remaining 16 ounces of chicken broth. Adjust seasonings to taste; add more salt and rock sugar, as preferred. The *pho* broth should be savory and slightly salty to balance the bland rice noodles. About 30 minutes before the *pho* broth is ready, add the *bò viên* meatballs if using. When the broth is done, discard the chicken parts still in the stockpot.

TO PREPARE THE NOODLES: Rinse the noodles in cold water and set them aside. Bring a large pot of water to a boil and, working in batches, dip the noodles into the boiling water for 10 to 20 seconds, stirring them until just tender and to keep them from tangling. Drain. (They are cooked separately because if dropped in the *pho* all at once, they would be soggy by the time they were served.)

TO SERVE THE *PHO*: Place about 2 cups of cooked noodles in each of 8 large soup bowls. Place a few slices of brisket, sliced raw eye-of-round, and poached chicken breast on the noodles. Garnish with sliced onions, green onions, cilantro, and black pepper to taste, then spoon 2 to 3 cups very hot broth and *bò viên* meatballs (optional) into each bowl. Season each bowl of *pho* with about ½ to 1 tablespoon fish sauce, or to taste before serving.

Guests can top the soup at the table with bean sprouts, Thai basil and *culantro*, chile slices, fresh limes for juice, pickled onions, and additional fish sauce to taste. Sriracha sauce and hoisin sauce are optional.

HALIMA MOHAMED
SOMALIA

Halima Mohamed, a mother of six, knew first-hand how difficult it can be for Somali women to find work in the United States. As a refugee from war-torn Somalia, she and her family fled to Kenya, where they spent seven years in the Otanga refugee camp before seeking refuge in the United States in 1997. There she found that many worksites were not accessible to Somali women who did not speak English or who did not drive. Many businesses simply would not hire women who wore hijabs. As sisters Halima and Mariam watched other Somali families struggle, they turned to what they knew—food—and envisioned a business where Somali women could thrive while sharing their culture through food from their homeland.

Sambusas were their food of choice. These triangular pastries, stuffed with fillings and spices—cumin, coriander, turmeric, and red chile peppers—are carefully hand-folded and lightly deep-fried. Though they resemble Indian *samosas*, they have different fillings and sizes. Halima and Mariam grew up making them, as did other Somali women.

Halima Mohamed

Wash Your Hands!
AND JUSTICE FOR ALL

"Everyone makes them," Halima says. "Everyone has their own recipe." *Sambusas* are made most often for special celebrations and holidays, in particular, *iftar*, the meal eaten after sunset to break the daily fast during the Muslim holiday of Ramadan.

The vision of starting a business was more challenging than expected. Initially operating from a church kitchen, the workspace was small, and food preparation was time-consuming. A day's work produced only 120 of the pastries, which were far too few to be commercially viable. Then Mariam and business partner Matt Glover located a food bank (Volunteers Enlisted to Assist People, or VEAP) that provided access to a commercial kitchen in Bloomington and, in 2016, Hoyo (Somali for "mother") opened its doors, with a logo featuring outstretched arms to represent Somali women.

Hoyo logo

Since its incorporation, Hoyo has employed thirty-five Somali women, and for many of them it was their first job in the United States. It currently has a team of eighteen people working full-time, nine of them Somali mothers, who together produce 3,000 to 3,500 *sambusas* per day.

The Hoyo kitchen today is a joyful place; hijabs are welcome, as are Somali language and mothers. During a visit, the team members were hard at work, hand-folding the two varieties of *sambusas*, beef and lentil. A daughter of one of the mothers joined the team later, continuing the tradition that began decades earlier.

"People are laughing and talking, but still we finish the job," says Halima. "They do the job better than anyone. Nothing is wrong with joy at work." In addition to the *sambusas*, Hoyo makes a dipping sauce, called "*basbaas*." The *sambusas* are available in the freezer section of more than forty local co-ops and supermarkets, and the *basbaas* is available on Amazon as well. Hoyo also partners with more than a dozen Minnesota school districts to provide students with this popular lunch item.

Halima believes that cooking and sharing food is a way to share her culture, and she does so with her traditional food wherever she can: at home, at her work at a nursing home, and through Hoyo. Her goal is to find a bigger production facility for Hoyo and expand.

"We take something they know and are good at, and now we make a living," she says of Hoyo. The *sambusas* recipes for the business originated with Halima, who shares them here.

Mahadsanid! Thank you!

Sambusas (Fried Pastry with Savory Filling)

Makes a varied amount, depending on size

FILLING

1 pound ground beef

1 medium onion, diced

1 to 2 garlic cloves, minced

1 teaspoon salt

1 teaspoon ground coriander

1 teaspoon ground cumin

1 teaspoon red pepper flakes

Dash of ground turmeric

WRAPPER

2¾ cups flour

2 teaspoons neutral vegetable oil, such as canola

½ teaspoon salt

1 tablespoon flour

Vegetable oil, for frying

NOTE: The staff at Hoyo use a tortilla press to make the wrappers for the *sambusas*, but they can be rolled out easily at home.

TO PREPARE THE FILLING: Brown the ground beef in a large skillet over medium heat and drain it, leaving a little fat. Sauté the onion in the same pan until translucent. Add the garlic, 1 teaspoon salt, coriander, cumin, red pepper flakes and turmeric. Cook for about 3 minutes while stirring, until thoroughly mixed

TO PREPARE THE WRAPPER: In a large bowl, mix together 2¾ cups flour, 1¼ cups water, oil, and ½ teaspoon salt. Form into balls of dough about 2 to 3 inches in diameter. Set aside to rest for 20 minutes with a towel over the top, so the dough does not dry out.

Sprinkle a little flour on the work surface to keep the dough from sticking. Take out 1 ball of dough and use a rolling pin to roll the ball into a flat circle with a 10- to 16-inch diameter. (The size will determine how big a *sambusa* is created.) Repeat with remaining balls.

(recipe continues on page 138)

Sambusas

Cut the flattened circles into quarters, making triangular-shaped pieces. Warm each of the flattened pieces over medium heat in a skillet to dry the wrapper a little, about 1 minute on each side. These wrappers need to be pliable, so do not make the wrappers crispy.

TO ASSEMBLE *SAMBUSAS*: Mix 1 tablespoon water and 1 tablespoon flour in a small bowl to create a paste. Fold a triangular wrapper piece into a cone shape and secure the edge with the flour paste. Place 1 tablespoon to ¼ cup of the filling inside the cone. (The amount will vary depending on the size of the wrapper.) Fold the top of the cone to close it into a triangular shape. Seal the edge with the flour paste.

Heat 1 quart of oil to 350°F in a deep fryer or a deep, heavy pot over high heat. There should be enough oil to submerge the wrappers. To test the temperature of the oil, drop a 1-inch cube of bread into the oil; it should brown in about 50 seconds. Fry both sides of the *sambusas*, about 1½ minutes on each side, until golden brown all over. Remove and drain on paper towels. Serve with *Basbaas*, or other condiment.

Basbaas (Green Dipping Sauce)

Makes 1 cup

- 1 medium onion, roughly chopped
- 5 medium jalapeños (remove seeds to reduce heat), roughly chopped
- 2½ tablespoons freshly squeezed lemon juice (about ½ lemon)
- ½ cup loosely packed chopped cilantro leaves and stems
- 1 large garlic clove, minced
- 1 teaspoon salt
- ½ teaspoon freshly ground black pepper

In a food processor or blender, combine the onion, jalapeños, lemon juice, cilantro, garlic, salt, and pepper. Purée until smooth.

Use immediately or store in an airtight container in the refrigerator. The potency of the hot sauce will lessen after a few days. The sauce works well as an accompaniment to *sambusas*, meat, or vegetables.

jalapeños

HAYDEE
EL SALVADOR

Haydee spent most of her life in San Salvador, the capital of El Salvador. As a lawyer, she worked many years in the police investigative force, as did her husband. Both always had a gun on their hip as they worked in a country ripped apart by brutality. "It was very hard," Haydee says now. She lost many coworkers to violence, and friends mourned the loss of family members. Haydee and her husband fought back, sending many criminals to jail. Death threats to her family followed, as did the presence of gang members at her home, which led to Haydee's decision to have her family leave the country for their safety.

Her approach was to use a U.S. visa to visit a family member in California. Haydee wanted a legal route to stay in the United States, but when she talked to a Los Angeles lawyer about immigration, he said the cost would be $14,000, which her family could not afford. She prayed, "God, I don't have money to pay for lawyers. I don't know what I can do. Give me an answer." Then her phone notification pinged. She had a message from a childhood friend, who knew Haydee was in the United States. She invited Haydee's family to stay with her in Minnesota and talked

Haydee

with Haydee about different volunteer organizations in the state that help families with immigration issues. “And I said, ‘Oh God, you respond very fast,’” Haydee recalls. “It was a miracle.”

Once in Minnesota, Haydee found the Advocates for Human Rights, which connected her to a volunteer lawyer at the University of Minnesota. With Haydee’s documentation and the help of clinic students and lawyers, her family applied for asylum and obtained it five years later. She and her family are very grateful to all the people who helped with the asylum case and gave them opportunities. They are very happy, too, because the family has a new member, a corgi puppy named Wilson.

In the meantime, the family experienced another miracle. Haydee and her family lived in an apartment that had disruptive neighbors next door. Her son said, “I want one home, one house, one bed.” Once again, Haydee searched online, and this time found Habitat for Humanity. They offered to help if Haydee could come up with $6,000 for a real estate closing. As Haydee’s family did not have those funds, she turned to prayer. When a hailstorm hit and their family car was damaged, a co-worker of Haydee’s husband directed them to their insurance agent. The resulting repair funds went toward the house.

Today Haydee and her family miss the beauty and food of their home country. Though they did not return, they bring El Salvador here. One of their favorite ways is to cook the food of their homeland. *Pupusas* are the signature dish, and in El Salvador, residents buy them from restaurants called *pupuserias*, which they frequent every weekend. “Or, if you were lucky enough, a couple times a week,” recalls Haydee’s son. These delightful pockets of filling—zucchini or carrot, chicken or cheese—are wrapped in masa dough and heated on a griddle. “The *pupusas* cannot be missing the natural tomato sauce and the *curtido* of cabbage and still be *pupusas*,” says Haydee. Working with the dough takes time to master, though these are delicious regardless of their final look. There is no limit to the various fillings that can be used.

Pupusas (Filled Corn Cakes)

Makes 9 to 10

NOTE: This recipe can easily be doubled. *Pupusas* are the national dish of El Salvador, where they are prepared in an almost infinite number of combinations. Make the tomato sauce first followed by the *curtido* and filling options, before you assemble the *pupusas* themselves.

NATURAL TOMATO SAUCE

Makes about 3 cups

- 4 to 5 medium tomatoes, cored and left whole
- ½ mild or sweet green chile or bell pepper, seeded and roughly chopped
- 1 jalapeño pepper, stemmed and seeded, optional
- ½ medium onion
- 2 fresh garlic cloves, peeled and left whole
- 2 teaspoons salt
- ¼ teaspoon granulated sugar
- Dash of freshly ground black pepper

Put 1¼ cups water and the tomatoes, chile or bell pepper, jalapeño (optional), onion, and garlic in a pot and bring to a boil, uncovered, over medium-high heat. Reduce the heat to low and simmer, stirring occasionally, until tomato skins loosen and vegetables are soft, about 10 to 12 minutes. Use tongs to remove the tomato skins and discard them. Transfer all contents of the pot, including the liquid, into a blender and add the salt, sugar, and black pepper. Carefully purée (as the liquid is hot) until mostly smooth. Pour the sauce into a container, skim off and discard any foam, and let the sauce come to room temperature.

CURTIDO (CABBAGE SLAW)

Makes about 2 quarts

- 1 (14-ounce) package shredded cabbage, green or tricolor (about 6 cups)
- 3 medium carrots, grated or cut in fine julienne
- ¼ small onion, cut into thin slices
- 1 tablespoon fresh oregano, or 1 teaspoon dried
- 1 cup apple cider vinegar
- 2 teaspoons salt

Bring 4 cups of water to a boil in a large pot over medium-high heat. Add the cabbage and cook for a minute or two, until the cabbage begins to soften. Drain the cabbage and place it in a large bowl. Add the carrots, onion, and oregano.

In a smaller bowl, mix the apple cider vinegar and salt with 2 cups water. Adjust flavors to taste and pour over the vegetables. Set aside.

FILLINGS

CHEESE ONLY: Use 8 to 16 ounces grated cheese (mozzarella or other cheese that melts well), at room temperature. If you wish, mix in finely sliced fresh basil or other herbs.

ZUCCHINI AND CHEESE: Grate 1 large zucchini (about 2 cups) and pat dry with paper towels. Add 3 cups grated cheese, 1 teaspoon salt, and 1 tablespoon water. Knead the ingredients together for about 5 minutes, making a firm but pliable mixture.

CARROT AND CHEESE: 2 medium carrots, grated and cooked in 2 teaspoons oil and 1 to 2 tablespoons water, with ¼ teaspoon turmeric, 1 teaspoon salt and ½ teaspoon black pepper, until tender. Knead in 2 cups grated cheese, if preferred.

Mix and match your favorite options and be creative with other fillings. Try cooked and shredded chicken, mashed pinto or black beans, or sautéed mushrooms.

MASA DOUGH

Makes 9 to 10 *pupusas*

---

3 cups masa flour

2 teaspoons neutral vegetable oil, such as canola

Filling for *pupusas* (see above)

NOTE: Look for masa flour, also called masa harina, such as Maseca brand, in supermarkets and Mexican specialty markets.

TO PREPARE MASA DOUGH: Mix the flour and 3¼ cups water in a large bowl using clean or gloved hands. Continue kneading the dough inside the bowl, using strong pressure, for at least 5 minutes. Add up to ¼ cup more water, as needed. The dough should have a soft consistency, somewhat like mashed potatoes.

TO ASSEMBLE *PUPUSAS*: Set a dry, flat *comal*, griddle, or skillet on medium-high heat. In a small dish, combine 1 cup warm water and 2 teaspoons oil. Dip your fingers in the mixture to wet your hands. Take ½ cup of masa dough (about the size of a small apple) and form it into a ball. Press it into a disk, then clap it back and forth between your hands until it is about ¼-inch thick. If the disk tears, form a new ball and start over. Add a little more flour if the dough is sticky.

Holding the disk on one upturned palm, use the other hand to place 1 to 2 tablespoons of filling in the center. Close your fist to make a ball around the filling, and with the other hand pinch the edges to seal.

Pupusas with *Curtido* and Natural Tomato Sauce

Gently twist off the excess dough at the seam of the ball. Put the excess dough back in the bowl for later use. Then press your hands together to flatten the filled disk until it's 5 inches in diameter and ½ inch thick. Gently brush a bit of the oiled water on each side. Place the *pupusas* on the heated surface and cook, flipping occasionally, until they are firm and dry, with browned spots, about 5 minutes on each side.

TO SERVE *PUPUSAS*: Have some Natural Tomato Sauce and *Curtido* at the table to top the *pupusas*.

YIA VANG

HMONG

Yia Vang didn't realize his life was different from the other kids at school. Despite having spent his first years at Ban Vinai, a Thai refugee camp, he didn't think about the word "refugee." The world he knew best was centered on a traditional Hmong household in a closely knit Hmong community. It was not until college that Yia began to consider that his life had been unlike others. He began to ask himself, "What does it mean to grow up as a refugee or immigrant?" Searching for answers led him back to his parents and their table.

During the Vietnam War, Yia's father, Nhia Lor, had been recruited at the age of twelve to work with the United States as part of the Secret Guerrilla Unit (SGU), a Central Intelligence Agency (CIA) operation. Nhia and his brothers were trained to locate downed planes and pilots in the jungles of Laos. In Yia's words, "My father served this country before he ever set foot here." Yia's uncles and grandfather died in the CIA-directed "secret war" and, when the United States pulled out of Vietnam, its Hmong allies were placed at risk. Nhia, like many others, had no choice but to flee. He gathered what he could carry, pointed his compass south, and started walking, with the hope that there would be a place for him in a refugee camp.

Nhia trekked through the jungles of Laos for two months to the banks of the Mekong River, crossing at night on a bamboo raft. He finally reached Ban Vinai and stayed there for eleven years. Nhia got married at Ban Vinai in 1977, and Yia and his siblings were born there. The United States finally honored its promise to the Hmong to provide citizenship for their service during the war, and Yia's family came to the United States in 1988, when he was five years old. Yia became a citizen in 2021.

Yia Vang

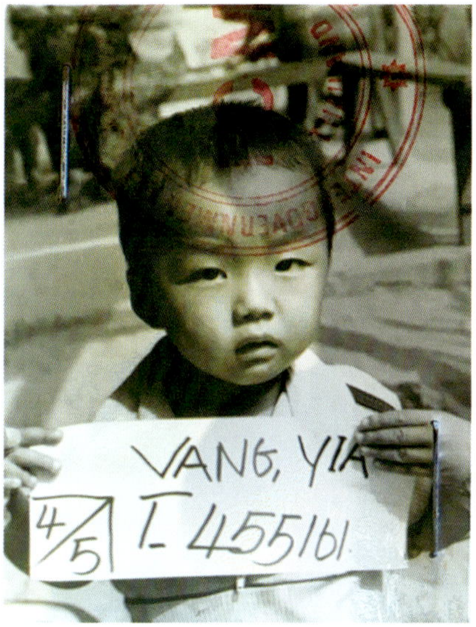

When Yia's family came to the United States, they had nothing: no land, no property. All they had were recipes from home, which were their legacy. "Food is our cultural DNA," he says. "Food tells our story. Food is our road map of our people and our culture."

Yia, whose name means "iron skillet" in Hmong, is proud of his heritage. He is humbled by the tremendous sacrifices his parents made to provide him with a future and teach him life lessons. "My dad was always there for me," Yia says. "He had a second-grade education and worked ten to twelve hours a day in a woodshop. At the end of the day, he took me fishing, and then started all over at 5 a.m. the next day."

But that understanding took a while for him. "I was a kid who was embarrassed of my dad, who never spoke English—and still doesn't," he says. "I didn't have white friends over. I was ashamed. As an adult, I'm now fighting for redemption."

The legacy of his parents continues through Yia's cooking, as well as his work on television. His restaurant Vinai is a love letter to his parents, one of hope, duty, honor, and respect for those who have made so many sacrifices. He hopes that others will see these strong Hmong traditions in his food. Vinai made the Best New Restaurant lists locally and nationally when it opened in 2024. He is also a James Beard Foundation finalist and semifinalist. In addition, Yia runs Union Hmong Kitchen, a hub for catering, in-home meals, and food operations in sports stadiums.

The dish that best reflects his heritage is Braised Pork with Hmong Mustard Greens. "This recipe is home," he says. "It is my mom. We eat this dish every day. Ninety-nine percent of the time a pot is on the stove in every Hmong household." Traditionally, the meat is served with rice and hot sauce, with the broth poured over the rice.

"It is foundational," Yia says. "It is love. It is heritage, and it is Hmong."

Braised Pork with Hmong Mustard Greens

Braised Pork with Hmong Mustard Greens

Serves 6

Yia Vang says there's nothing better to eat on a cold day than this combo.

- 2 to 3 pounds pork bones (use neck and ribs) all with some meat on the bones
- 3 full-size lemongrass stalks
- About a 4-inch chunk of fresh ginger root, peeled and cut into 3 pieces
- Salt, to taste
- 1 big bunch Hmong mustard greens, well washed (see Note)
- Hot cooked sticky (also known as sweet or glutinous) rice

NOTE: Yia notes that Hmong mustard greens are not the same as the familiar mustard greens in the supermarket (buy Hmong mustard greens at a Hmong market), and that *yu choy* can be used instead, though it's not exactly the same.

Put the bones in a large stock pot and cover with water. Bring to a boil over high heat, then reduce the heat to low. Add the lemongrass, ginger root, and salt, and simmer for 35 to 45 minutes, skimming off any film that appears. For the last 15 minutes, add the mustard greens—the more the better. Salt to taste. Serve the meat, broth, and greens with sticky rice and with Tiger Bite Sauce on the side.

Tiger Bite Sauce

Makes about ½ cup

- 1 teaspoon canola oil
- 1 small shallot, finely chopped
- 4 garlic cloves, finely chopped
- 2 to 4 Thai chiles, seeded and finely chopped (start with 2 and add more for desired heat)
- ½ cup finely chopped fresh cilantro
- 1 teaspoon fish sauce
- 1 tablespoon oyster sauce
- ¼ cup freshly squeezed lime juice
- Salt and freshly ground black pepper, to taste

Using mortar and pestle, add the ingredients one by one, working each ingredient in until a paste forms: oil, shallot, garlic, chiles, cilantro, fish sauce, oyster sauce, lime juice, and salt and pepper to taste.

Store in the refrigerator.

Thai chiles

KITCHENS OF CELEBRATION

No matter the special occasion, we celebrate the moment by sharing a meal. Shereen Fakier knows that food makes a difference when trying to connect with others, and she does so with her blend of South African and Indian food. Omar Guevara-Soto brings out the traditional Mexican sweet *tres leches* cake when he has reason to get together with others. Nazneen Khatoon often gathers friends and extended family around the table for Indian fare. Mila finds delight in making her grandchildren's favorite Bosnian delicacy. Tenia Kalogeropoulou celebrates the Christmas holidays with sweets and tradition from Greece and beyond. For Yan Mo, it's the Chinese New Year that brings great joy and treasured rice cake. All invite you to share their cherished celebration foods, fresh from your own kitchen.

SHEREEN FAKIER

SOUTH AFRICA

Shereen Fakier is a second-generation South African. Her grandparents migrated there from a small rural community in Maharashtra, India. Shereen's grandfathers first left for South Africa to work in the coal mines under British rule. After traveling back and forth between the two countries, they brought their families to South Africa.

Growing up in South Africa near the end of apartheid, Shereen witnessed the segregation around her and wanted to learn more of the world beyond this system. At age seventeen, she left her home country for Vancouver Island, Canada, to attend Lester B. Pearson College, which is a part of the United World Colleges Organization. She says the school was founded to "bring students together from as many countries as we can, so they can all work together, for world peace and understanding, creating a global community." The school had students from ninety different countries, and friendships that Shereen made during that time continue to this day.

She moved to the United States more than twenty years ago as her

Shereen Fakier

husband, Adil, was working there at the time. He is South African, with Malaysian heritage. They planned to stay only briefly, but two decades later they are still in the United States, where Shereen works as an occupational therapist in neurological rehabilitation. Their family shares dual South African and U.S. citizenship. "South Africa is still very much a part of our identity," Shereen says.

And that includes its food. "In my mom's generation, there weren't very many opportunities for Indian women in apartheid South Africa," Shereen says. "She and her siblings had all been cooking since they were teenagers, so she finds a lot of meaning in the kitchen. When we go home, she just wants to feed us. She wants to feed everybody, so it's always a lot of eating there."

Though she grew up watching her grandmother, mother, and aunts in the kitchen, Shereen says she couldn't boil an egg when she married. In the United States, she began to crave the foods she grew up eating and couldn't find those from the region in India where her family is from, not even in Indian restaurants. "I'm sure this mirrors my grandmother's experience when she first came to South Africa," says Shereen. "She couldn't necessarily find the ingredients, and she had to figure it out."

Through many calls to her mother, and by trial and error, Shereen began to learn. Though her mother and grandmother do not use recipes, Shereen does. "I wanted to have that connection to my grandmother and pass it on to my daughter," she says. Shereen remembers when the PTA at her children's school asked for suggestions on how to get families of color and immigrant families to be more involved. "If you share a meal, people will show up," Shereen says. "Food breaks down a barrier that you can't otherwise do."

Shereen serves *samoosas* during the month-long Muslim observance of Ramadan, with her mother's tamarind chutney. "Traditionally, in the Malaysian and Indian communities, *samoosas* are eaten at every gathering," Shereen says. "If there isn't a *samoosa* there, it's not a celebration." The challenge with the *samoosas* is the folding of them into a triangular shape. Unlike when Shereen learned how to make them, today's cooks can find tutorials on the internet to learn the process.

Shereen also shares a recipe for her grandmother's version of chicken curry. "I don't think my mom or my grandmother even think about how you make that recipe, they just make it," says Shereen. "I still look at the recipe."

The dish takes her back home. "It reminds me of my house," says Shereen. "It reminds me of my community. It's just a very strong connection. We make many kinds of curries, but the chicken curry specifically reminds me of my community and of home."

Chicken *Samoosas* (Fried Pastry with Savory Filling)

Makes 50 or more *samoosas*

NOTE: Plan ahead if using chicken breasts, which need to be prepared in advance. Indian chile powder is found at Indian grocery stores and is different from other chile powder.

- Vegetable oil
- 1 teaspoon whole cumin seeds
- 1 medium onion, finely chopped (about 1 cup)
- 2 pounds cooked chicken breasts, diced, or raw ground chicken (see Note)
- 1 teaspoon minced fresh garlic
- 1 teaspoon minced fresh ginger root, peeled
- 1 teaspoon Indian red chile powder (see Note)
- 1 teaspoon ground coriander
- 1 teaspoon ground cumin
- 1 Thai green chile, seeded and finely chopped
- ⅓ cup freshly chopped cilantro
- ¼ cup freshly chopped mint
- 1 tablespoon flour
- 2 packages egg roll wrappers (8-inches square, with 25 square sheets each)

TO MAKE THE FILLING: Heat 1 tablespoon oil in a skillet over medium heat and add the cumin seeds and onion. Stir until golden, then add the chicken, garlic, ginger, chile powder, coriander, and ground cumin. Continue cooking and stirring for several minutes or, if using raw chicken, until the chicken is cooked through. Make sure any moisture has mostly evaporated (a wet mixture will make for a soggy *samoosa* that will burn when fried). Remove from the heat and let the filling cool. Once the filling is cool, toss in the green chile, cilantro, and mint.

TO ASSEMBLE THE *SAMOOSAS*: Make a paste to seal the *samoosas* by combining the flour and 2 tablespoons water in a small dish (this should be spreadable but not wet or runny) and set aside. Cut the stack of egg roll wrappers into 3 equal strips. Wrap the stack loosely in a damp cloth while you work, to avoid drying out.

Take a strip and lay it in front of you vertically. Use your finger to apply a bit of flour paste in a line along the lower third of the right side of the strip. Bring the bottom left corner up to the right edge, aligning the sides, to create a triangle. Take the triangle and fold it to the left side, which will result in a "pocket" in the strip. Add 2 teaspoons of the filling in the pocket. Press the top edge of the pocket and fold the triangle back to the right side, and repeat this process, going back and forth with the triangle to the end of the strip. With your finger, dab some of the flour paste at the top edge of the strip and fold it over the triangle, pressing the edge with paste so it adheres. Set aside and repeat with the remaining strips and filling.

TO COOK THE *SAMOOSAS*: Line a plate with paper towels. If using a deep fryer, heat 2 to 3 cups oil at 350°F. If using a frying pan, heat about ¼ cup oil. Place the *samoosas* in the hot oil and fry them until they are crisp and golden in color, for about a few minutes. Do not let them get

too dark. Transfer the *samoosas* to the plate, and serve hot with the *Amli* Chutney.

TO FREEZE THE *SAMOOSAS*: Place the uncooked *samoosas* in a single layer on a baking sheet and freeze them. Once frozen, store them in the freezer in a container or freezer-safe bags. To heat them, fry them as indicated, without thawing them first. Shereen prefers to freeze *samoosas* before deep-frying them.

Amli Chutney (Tamarind Dipping Sauce)

Makes 4 or more cups

- 150 grams tamarind pulp (sold dried, in a square or rectangular block packaged in plastic; choose seedless if available; see Note)
- ½ cup red chile flakes (this seems like a lot, but the ketchup mellows it out)
- 2 tablespoons pickle masala spice (see Note)
- ½ cup granulated sugar
- 4 teaspoons sesame seeds
- 2½ cups ketchup
- 1 cup white vinegar
- 2 tablespoons vegetable oil
- 2 teaspoons mustard seeds
- A sprig of fresh curry leaves (about 8 leaves), available at Indian grocery stores (sold in plastic bags in the produce section)
- Salt, to taste

Place the tamarind pulp in 1½ cups boiling water. As it cooks, stir it to break up the block, until the pulp loosens and thickens. Press the tamarind pulp firmly through a metal mesh sieve with the back of a spoon to remove the strings, seeds and tough parts. Scrape the pulp off the bottom of the sieve into a bowl as it comes through. You will need to press very firmly, repeatedly, to get as much pulp as possible. You should have about ½ cup of strained tamarind. If you have more, please use it!

Place the tamarind pulp, chile flakes, pickle masala spice, sugar, sesame seeds, ketchup, and vinegar in a pot over medium heat, and cook for about 10 minutes.

Warm the oil in a skillet over medium heat and add the mustard seeds and curry leaves. Once the oil is fragrant and the seeds stop sputtering (just a few minutes), add to the tamarind sauce. Season with salt to taste. Once cool, store in a sterile glass bottle and refrigerate (it makes a large quantity and can last quite a while in the refrigerator).

NOTE: Find tamarind pulp in Indian and Mexican grocery stores. Chunks of tamarind pulp come in different sizes, but will only be described in grams on the package. You will need to cut off 150 grams, which you can calculate based on the size of the chunk you buy and its weight. Pickle masala spice is available at Indian grocery stores or online.

mustard seeds

Chicken Curry

Serves 6

- 3 tablespoons vegetable oil or ghee
- 1 medium yellow onion, sliced
- 3 cardamom seeds
- 4 whole cloves
- 1 cinnamon stick
- 1½ teaspoons minced fresh ginger root
- 1½ teaspoons fresh minced garlic (1 to 2 cloves)
- 2 pounds boneless and skinless chicken thighs or chicken tenders
- 1 teaspoon salt
- ½ teaspoon ground turmeric
- 1 teaspoon ground cumin
- 1 teaspoon Indian red chile powder, less if you don't like heat (see Note)
- 2 teaspoons ground coriander
- 2 teaspoons ground fennel
- 1½ teaspoons garam masala
- 1 teaspoon paprika
- 1 to 2 large tomatoes, grated, divided
- 1 Thai green chile, seeded and chopped
- 1 tablespoon tomato paste
- 4 to 5 unpeeled Yukon Gold potatoes, or other medium-sized waxy yellow potato, quartered
- 1 handful of fresh cilantro, chopped
- Hot cooked basmati rice

Warm the vegetable oil (or ghee) in a large pot over medium heat. Add the onion, cardamom seeds, cloves, and cinnamon stick and cook until golden and caramelized, about 10 minutes. Using a mortar and pestle, mix the ginger and garlic into a paste. Add the chicken, ginger/garlic paste, and salt and cook to brown the meat. Add the turmeric, cumin, chile powder, coriander, fennel, garam masala, and paprika. Mix to coat the chicken with the spices.

Add about ⅓ cup hot water and continue to cook the chicken for 5 minutes. Meanwhile, grate a tomato over a bowl to catch the juice and pulp, discarding the skin that remains attached to the stem end. Add the tomato juice and pulp, the green chile, and tomato paste. Reduce the heat to low and simmer slowly, covered, until the chicken is almost cooked through, about 10 to 15 minutes. Add the potatoes, cover the pan, and cook until the potatoes are tender, about 20 to 25 minutes more, stirring occasionally to scrape the bottom of the pan. If more liquid is needed, add a bit of water or another grated tomato. Garnish with cilantro before serving with basmati rice.

NOTE: Indian chile powder is found at Indian grocery stores and is different from other chile powder.

OMAR GUEVARA-SOTO

MEXICO

Omar Guevara-Soto discovered his passion for making good food as a young boy, when he could not wait to get to his grandmother's restaurant each day after school. Located in the middle of Puebla, Mexico, the restaurant sat on a street that led to a market. From a tiny side door in the alley, Omar's family sold tamales and *atole*, a hot chocolate corn drink, to the vendors who began making their way at three o'clock every morning. His grandmother was concerned about the well-being of the vendors and of her employees. She also took great care with the food. "I have vivid memories of my grandmother sitting and sorting through the food scraps from the day and putting them in buckets," Omar says. "She would inspect even the banana peels that would feed the massive clay *mole* poblano pot, because her passion was food." Omar found it fascinating to see the food world at work.

As a teenager, Omar was recruited by the YMCA to come to Minnesota for the Camp Warren experience in Eveleth. Following his time as a camper, he became an employee, returning summer after summer. After

Omar Guevara-Soto

college in Mexico, Omar returned to Minnesota to attend Le Cordon Bleu culinary school. He knocked on doors near his home and got a job working for Twin Cities chef Lucia Watson at her Lucia's Restaurant in Minneapolis. Like his grandmother, Lucia cared for her staff, her vendors, and her food. From Lucia, Omar learned all about the Twin Cities food system. When school finished, he needed to return to Mexico, but soon after began working with a restaurant group that was opening venues across the United States. After hosting many a conga line, Omar decided to move on from the tourist party atmosphere. He obtained his green card (permanent residency to live and work in the United States) quickly and returned to the Twin Cities.

Omar began working with Ann Kim, a Korean immigrant chef and James Beard Award winner, whose work has influenced the Twin Cities food scene. She sponsored a pizza garden for the middle school in her Minneapolis neighborhood and provided funds so schools could offer salad bars. Omar wondered how it was possible in a First World country to have so much hunger and lack of access to fresh food. "It was a very naïve question," he says, but he started looking into it. When a job opened in food service for the Minneapolis Public Schools, he took it.

As assistant director of culinary and wellness services, Omar helped lead a quiet revolution, fundamentally changing the way school lunch is made. When he began in 2013, most Minneapolis public schools did not have kitchens. Instead, schools warmed prepackaged lunch trays to serve to children. Today, most Minneapolis schools have kitchens, and a lot of cooking-from-scratch cooking goes on. This takes tenacity and creativity, as the National School Lunch Act specifies detailed requirements for every meal, with limited funds per student to cover labor and ingredients costs. The Minneapolis district has joined other Midwestern districts to gain purchasing power for some ingredients, including quality chicken. Other districts from across the country send staff to shadow and learn from the Minneapolis team.

Omar pays his good fortune forward by making good food and making it available. When one hard-working mom took him to task for introducing her child to fresh foods she could not afford, he invited her to lean into the schools, allowing them to feed her child breakfast, lunch, and dinner. And Omar is not done yet. In 2023, he was awarded a Bush Foundation Fellowship to enhance his leadership skills and address the growing problem of food insecurity.

Omar shares the recipe for *Tres Leches* Cake, a dessert his grandmother made, filled with delicious sweetness. "It is this recipe," he says, "that brings me home."

Tres Leches Cake (Three Milk Cake)

Makes 12 or more servings

CAKE

Cooking spray

1 cup flour

1½ teaspoons baking powder

¼ teaspoon salt

5 eggs, separated

1 cup granulated sugar, divided

1 teaspoon vanilla extract

⅓ cup whole milk

TOPPING

1 (12-ounce) can evaporated milk

1 (14-ounce) can sweetened condensed milk

¼ cup heavy cream

½ cup whole milk

1 teaspoon rum or whiskey, optional

ICING

2 cups heavy cream

3 tablespoons granulated sugar

Raspberries or other favorite fruit, or cinnamon sugar (see Note), for decoration

NOTE: Cinnamon sugar is easy to make, with equal amounts of ground cinnamon and granulated sugar.

TO MAKE THE CAKE: Preheat the oven to 350°F. Coat the bottom and sides of a 9- by 13-inch pan with cooking spray. In a large bowl, whisk together the flour, baking powder, and salt, and set aside.

In the bowl of an electric mixer, beat the egg yolks and ¾ cup sugar on medium-high speed until the mixture is pale. Add ⅓ cup whole milk and the vanilla extract and beat until fully incorporated.

Using a spatula, carefully fold the egg yolk mixture into the flour mixture, just until the dry ingredients are wet and combined.

Wash and dry the beaters for the electric mixer. Then use the mixer to whip the egg whites on medium speed until they are foamy, about 2 minutes. Increase the speed to medium-high and mix until soft peaks form, about 2 minutes. Increase the speed to high, and with the mixer running, gradually add the remaining ¼ cup sugar and whip until the meringue forms stiff, glossy (but not dry) peaks, about 2 to 3 minutes.

Using a spatula, carefully fold the meringue into the batter, until just combined. Pour the batter into the prepared baking pan, and even out the surface. Bake until a toothpick or fork inserted into the center of the cake comes out clean, about 35 to 40 minutes. Remove the cake from the oven and set it on a wire rack to cool to room temperature.

TO MAKE THE TOPPING: In a small saucepan over medium heat, combine the evaporated milk, condensed milk, ¼ cup heavy cream, ½ cup whole milk, and the rum or whiskey (optional). Whisk until combined and heated through; do not simmer or boil. Remove the saucepan from the heat and allow the topping to come to room temperature.

Using a fork, pierce the surface of the cooled cake many times. Slowly drizzle the topping over the top of the cake, making sure that it spreads as much as possible to the edges. Allow the cake to fully absorb

Tres Leches Cake

the topping. When the top of the cake looks dry, it's ready to be iced.

TO MAKE THE ICING: In the bowl of an electric mixer fitted with a whisk attachment, combine 2 cups heavy cream and 3 tablespoons sugar and whip on medium-high speed until the cream is thick. Spread the whipped cream in an even layer over the top of the cake. Decorate with fruit (raspberries are especially nice), or sprinkle with cinnamon sugar. Refrigerate the cake until ready to serve, then cut into squares for serving.

NAZNEEN KHATOON

INDIA

Nazneen Khatoon began her life in India, a country that emerged from British colonial rule in 1947 and chose to become a secular democracy. She fondly recalls the circle of her friends with diverse religious backgrounds: Hindus, Muslims, Sikhs, and Christians living next to each other in "peace, love and harmony," she says. That tradition has come under stress in recent times.

Nazneen had an arranged marriage at age eighteen, set up by her parents and elders in the community, according to the custom of that time. She and her husband, who was eight years older, immediately moved to Chicago, where he was pursuing his graduate education. "When I was first here, I was really a daredevil," Nazneen says. "I took the challenge very easy." The year was 1974, a time when Chicago did not have much of an Indian community. "I was really thrown into this wide ocean without anybody holding my hand," Nazneen says. She needed to find her way. Though she spoke English, she wasn't fluent. Once she found work, she picked up that proficiency simply by interacting with her colleagues.

Less than a year after they arrived, Nazneen and her husband moved to Minnesota, where he was a student for many years, ultimately becoming a pediatrician. While he pursued his education, Nazneen worked to support the family. She succeeded in the banking industry but found the demands of that schedule difficult to meet alongside the needs of her growing family. After a few months at home with her

Nazneen Khatoon

children, Nazneen began a new venture, setting up an office to provide supplemental nursing care to nursing homes. When Minnesota began a new Personal Care Assistant (PCA) program, Nazneen was ready with the right set of skills and relationships. She now has about one hundred employees and contracts with major local health plans. "I find that this was typical of immigrants who came here, who wanted to really establish themselves here," Nazneen says. "We were laser-focused. We were committed."

Through her work in the health-services industry, Nazneen has seen firsthand how strong the connection can be between food and community, and between food and home. So often an elder will ask if she knows someone in her network of home-health providers who can cook the food from the elder's homeland. "Right from your childhood, your palates get used to the food you're raised on," says Nazneen, who finds that those elders want to eat the foods they knew in their youth. To this day, her husband prefers fresh home-cooked Indian food, even something simple, over dining at restaurants.

Nazneen and her husband share their traditional Indian foods with others in many ways. That includes offering dinners for auction as fundraisers to support the Advocates for Human Rights. The unprecedented religious strife and persecution in India in recent years targeting Muslims, Christians, and Dalits have left Nazneen and her husband concerned for their birth country and interested in promoting human rights in India and throughout the world.

Nazneen expresses her thankfulness for having three children and eight grandchildren. Her family tries their best to pass on their home language. At school and with friends, the grandchildren speak English. But when they are at home, with their parents and grandparents, they speak the language of their home in India. "We speak Urdu," Nazneen says. Ever gracious, Nazneen offers a taste of her culture with this signature celebration dish of many layers of rice, lamb, and onions.

Achchhee bhookh! Enjoy your meal!

Hyderabadi Lamb dum Biryani

Serves 16

NOTE: Plan ahead, as the dish needs to be refrigerated for about 45 minutes. The name reflects a style of *biryani*, with basmati rice and lamb, that is from the city of Hyderabad, India. All the ingredients can be found at Indian grocery stores. Black jeera seeds are black cumin.

LAMB

2 pounds bone-in leg of lamb, with meat cut into ¾-inch cubes, saving the bones

2 tablespoons grated peeled fresh ginger root

2 tablespoons minced garlic

1 tablespoon meat tenderizer or papaya paste (either, for tenderizing meat)

1 teaspoon salt

2 teaspoons ground turmeric

2 teaspoons ground cayenne pepper

1 cinnamon stick

2 whole cloves

10 cardamom pods

Peanut oil or sunflower oil, for frying

1 large white onion, thinly sliced

5 tablespoons whole Greek yogurt

Freshly squeezed juice from 2 lemons

¼ cup freshly chopped mint

¼ cup freshly chopped cilantro

2 green chiles, seeded, if preferred, finely chopped

TO COOK THE LAMB: Lay the lamb pieces (meat and bones) in the bottom of a very large Dutch oven or large aluminum pan (such as one used to roast a turkey). Mash both the ginger root and garlic into paste and add to the pan. Add the meat tenderizer, salt, turmeric, cayenne pepper, 1 cinnamon stick, cloves, and 10 cardamom pods, and mix in with the meat with your hands.

In a sauté pan, heat 1 inch of oil to 350°F. Add the thinly sliced onions and fry until light golden and crisp. Remove from the oil and drain on paper towels. Set the oil aside and save a few of the fried onions for garnish when the dish is complete. Crush the remaining fried onions, add them to the meat and mix with your hands. Add the yogurt and mix again. Add the lemon juice and 2 tablespoons of the reserved oil. Cover the pan and refrigerate for 40 to 45 minutes, for the flavor to develop.

TO MAKE THE *BIRYANI*: While the meat is marinating, parboil the rice as if it were pasta, in 6 cups of salted boiling water, with 3 cardamom pods, 1 cinnamon stick, and black jeera seeds. After 10 minutes, when the rice is still crunchy in the middle, remove it from the heat and strain, reserving any water. Remove and discard the cardamom pods and cinnamon stick.

Preheat the oven to 350°F. Coat a large, deep baking dish or large aluminum disposable pan with cooking spray. Layer one-quarter of the rice on the bottom of the pan. In a small bowl, mix the ghee (or vegetable oil) with 1 cup of the reserved water and pour over the rice in the baking dish. Next, layer the marinated meat on top of the rice. Add the chopped mint, cilantro, and green chiles on top of the marinated meat.

Hyderabadi Lamb dum Biryani

BIRYANI

3 cups basmati rice

3 cardamom pods

1 cinnamon stick

1 teaspoon black jeera seeds (black cumin; see Note)

6 tablespoons ghee or vegetable oil

1 teaspoon saffron, boiled in 1 cup milk for 5 minutes

Naan, for serving

Now layer the remaining rice on top of the vegetables and pour the saffron and milk mixture over the top. Cover the dish in aluminum foil and bake for 40 to 50 minutes. Turn off the oven and leave the dish in the oven for about 15 minutes.

Remove the baking pan from the oven and remove the aluminum foil. Carefully mix the layer of rice and meat. Garnish with the fried onions and chopped cilantro. Serve with the *naan*. Add a simple Indian salad of chopped tomatoes, cucumber, red onions, a little bit of green chile, and lots of fresh cilantro, tossed with some lime juice and salt.

MILA
BOSNIA

Some memories are best left in the past. That's true for Mila, who was born in the town of Bijeljina, in northeastern Bosnia. Her country borders Serbia, Montenegro, and Croatia. All were part of the Socialist Federal Republic of Yugoslavia until its breakup in 1992, at which point Bosnia declared independence. The Bosnian War, which followed, lasted three years. Mila and her family fled their country during this time, traveling first to Germany and then coming to the United States in 2000. They joined her sister in Minnesota, who had immigrated there earlier.

Mila created a new life in Minnesota by always looking forward. "Life is not easy, but we must always keep trying," she says. Today she runs a housekeeping business, as well as helps her three grown children and grandchildren.

Though settled in Minnesota, Bosnia is not far from her mind. She has fond memories of her home country, surrounded by large gardens full of vegetables and flowers, in particular roses. Her mother made a favorite drink from the flower petals.

Mila shares two recipes from Bosnia that she makes for family and friends: Bosnian pita and *baklava*. Not to be confused with the flatbread of the same name, Bosnian pita is a traditional pastry made of handmade dough that is stretched paper-thin (think phyllo sheets) and stuffed with various fillings. She prefers one of spinach, green onions, and feta, but her pita can be filled with cheese alone or other ingredients. Mila says it's best made with Turkish or Bosnian pita flour, which makes the dough more stretchable. She prefers to bake it in a deep, round baking pan, although rectangular pans can also be used. The pita is generally served with homemade yogurt. Traditionally prepared for holidays at home, the pita is a staple at restaurants in Bosnia. Mila's grandchildren love this dish and ask her to make it again and again.

Her other recipe, for *baklava*, is a popular dessert made of layers of phyllo sweetened with honey and nuts. Though many countries claim *baklava* as theirs, Mila thinks the Bosnian version is best.

Spinach, Feta, and Green Onion Pita

Spinach, Feta, and Green Onion Pita

Makes 2 pitas (8 servings per 18-inch round pan; 12 pieces per 9- by 13-inch pan)

FILLING

2 bunches (about 1 pound) spinach, chopped

½ cup chopped green onions

1 cup feta cheese, diced

2 eggs, beaten

½ teaspoon salt

1 cup olive oil

PITA DOUGH

3½ cups Turkish or Burek flour (see Note)

1 teaspoon salt

Vegetable oil

NOTE: Turkish flour or Bosnian flour (such as the brand Pravi Zlatni Puder) makes a difference in this dish, allowing the dough to be more stretchable. It's available at Bosnian markets. If you don't want to make the pita dough, you could substitute phyllo for the pita dough (see the recipe that follows for *baklava*, that uses phyllo, for how to do the process with melted butter on each of the phyllo sheets). The filling and pita dough can be halved to make only a single pita.

TO MAKE THE FILLING: In a large bowl, combine the spinach, green onions, feta, eggs, ½ teaspoon salt, and olive oil. Mix well and set aside.

TO MAKE THE DOUGH: In a large bowl, combine the flour and 1 teaspoon salt. Add 1¼ to 1½ cups lukewarm water bit by bit, mixing until the mixture forms a dough. On a lightly floured work surface, knead the dough until it becomes quite stretchy, about 5 to 10 minutes. Split the dough into four pieces and press each piece by hand to flatten it into a disk. Add a little bit of vegetable oil to the bottom and sides of a pan or bowl large enough to hold the dough pieces and put the first flattened piece of dough in it.

Spread 1 to 2 tablespoons more vegetable oil (not too much) over the dough in the pan or bowl. Repeat to add the other three pieces of dough on top of the first. Let the dough rest for 5 to 10 minutes.

Preheat the oven to 400°F. Spread a thin layer of vegetable oil over a large work surface (the dough will be stretched to 3 feet in diameter). Remove one piece of dough from the pan or bowl and wipe off the excess oil with a paper towel. Flatten the piece of dough with your hands until it reaches a thickness of no more than about ¼ inch. Handle the dough, stretching it outward, over and over, until it is about 3 feet in diameter. If you're using a rectangular pan rather than a round one, stretch the dough into that shape. You might end up with a few holes in the dough, but don't worry about that. By the end, you should be able to see through the dough.

If using an 18-inch rimmed round pan, leave the stretched dough on the work surface. To make it easier to put the stretched dough in the round pan, lightly mark a circle about 12 inches in diameter in the center of the stretched dough. Using a knife, make even cuts from the edge of the stretched dough to the marked circle, creating wedges that look like spokes. Fold each wedge toward the marked circle. Place the dough in the pan.

If using a 9- by 13-inch pan, shape the dough into a rectangle and, as though there's a center line down the long side, fold over one long edge to the middle, and do the same with the other side. Then fold it once again. Size the dough to match the pan and place it in the pan, folding over extra dough where needed.

Repeat the stretching and folding with the second piece of dough.

TO FINISH THE PITA: Place half the filling mixture on top of the dough in the pan. Add the other piece of stretched dough, shaped to fit the pan, on top of the filling and pinch the edges of the pieces of dough together. Bake until the pita is a golden color, about 30 minutes. Remove the pan from the oven and let it cool down a bit. Cut into serving pieces and serve warm.

There will be two pieces of dough remaining to make another pita. Repeat the process or freeze the dough for later use (thaw in the refrigerator overnight before using).

Baklava

Makes 24 to 36 pieces

NOTE: Plan ahead, as the phyllo dough needs to thaw overnight in the refrigerator. The number of phyllo sheets varies by producer. Adapt the number to the recipe accordingly. This recipe requires a pastry brush.

- 1 (16-ounce) frozen package phyllo dough (about 40 sheets), thawed according to package directions
- 1¼ cups (2½ sticks) butter, melted, or more if needed
- 3 cups finely chopped walnuts, divided
- 1 cup granulated sugar
- ½ cup honey
- 2 tablespoons freshly squeezed lemon juice

Preheat the oven to 325°F. Brush the bottom and sides of a 9- by 13-inch baking pan with melted butter.

Unroll the phyllo dough and have a damp towel handy to cover the dough so it doesn't dry out. Trim the phyllo dough to fit the prepared baking pan.

Place 10 phyllo sheets, one at a time, into the prepared baking pan, lightly brushing the top of each sheet with butter once it's in the pan, before adding the next. Brush the top of the last phyllo sheet, as well. Keep the remaining phyllo covered with a damp towel at all times. Evenly spread about ¾ cup walnuts over the top sheet.

Then place an additional 10 phyllo sheets into the baking pan, brushing the top of each sheet with melted butter before adding the next.

(recipe continues on page 168)

Brush the top of the last phyllo sheet as well. Evenly spread about ¾ cup walnuts over the top sheet.

Repeat with 5 more buttered phyllo sheets, ending with ¾ cup walnuts on top, and repeat with another 5 sheets, ending with ¾ cup walnuts on top. Use the same method to add the remaining phyllo sheets and brush the top sheet with butter.

Use a sharp knife to cut the pastry into the shapes you prefer before baking (squares, rectangles, diamonds, etc.). Bake until the top is golden, about 90 minutes.

Meanwhile, in a medium saucepan over medium-high heat, combine the sugar, honey, lemon juice, and ¾ cup water. Bring to a boil, stirring until the sugar is dissolved. Reduce the heat to medium-low and boil an additional 4 minutes without stirring. Remove the saucepan from the heat and allow the syrup to cool while the *baklava* is baking.

When the *baklava* has finished baking, remove the pan from the oven and immediately spoon the cooled syrup evenly over the cuts in the *baklava* first and then drizzle the remaining syrup over the top of the pastry. Set the baking pan on a wire rack and let the *baklava* cool completely. Store the *baklava* in an airtight container at room temperature.

Baklava

TENIA KALOGEROPOULOU

GREECE

Tenia Kalogeropoulou was born in Athens, Greece, to a close family. Little did she know that, in the not-so-distant future, her family would stretch across three continents: Europe, North America, and Asia.

She attended school in Athens, deciding early to pursue a career in medicine. After graduating from high school, she moved to the United Kingdom, where she spent nine years in college and medical school, as well as a medical internship, before returning to Greece for a medical residency. Applicants for residencies sometimes have to wait for years for a spot in a Greek program. After two years without a position available, Tenia turned to the United States, where she was selected for a residency, a decision that changed the dynamics of her life.

Although she planned to return to Greece following her training, life intervened. She met her husband, a physician from India, while completing residencies in internal medicine and endocrinology. They married and started a family, and Minnesota, where they had flourishing medical practices, became home.

Tenia Kalogeropoulou

But that was not without challenges in a new country. Her life in the United States was very different from that in Greece. "In the United States, life is more hectic," Tenia says. "People don't just drop in. In Greece, life is more relaxed and spontaneous." Her biggest challenge was the distance from family and friends in Greece and India. Like many newcomers before her, Tenia found it difficult to meet people in Minnesota when not born here. She has embraced the international communities in Minnesota but has found that developing a feeling of belonging is not finished work. Rather, it is a work in progress.

With the strong pull of family, Tenia, her husband and their two children return each summer to Kefalonia, an island in the Ionian Sea, west of mainland Greece, where her mother's family has property. Her face lights up as she describes the houseful of family, where open doors, the laughter of children, and cousins running up and down the stairs are part of the daily commotion. And, of course, where everyone cooks.

"In both India and Greece, our focus is on family and hospitality," Tenia says. "Food is part of our culture. So is telling stories and sharing our traditions. It is part of our hospitality and makes people feel welcome."

As a mother, she does not limit her children to foods of Greek or Indian traditions. She wants her children to be exposed to foods from multiple cultures in an effort to make them more culturally aware. That's true during the Christmas holidays, when she bakes gingerbread cookies with her children, as well as her Greek cookies. "We celebrate every occasion," Tenia says. "We have many holidays where we make food and sweets that bring good wishes to the house."

One such recipe is for *Vasilopita*, a New Year's cake served for luck, that's part of the festivities that run from December 24 until January 6. On New Year's Eve, the family gathers and marks the occasion with heaping plates of chicken with tomato sauce and pasta, followed by the *Vasilopita*, which has a coin baked into it. Slices of the cake are passed out from the oldest family member to the youngest. The one who gets the slice with the coin will have good luck for the whole year. They also give out charms to everyone who attends. The holiday continues with card playing all night.

Tenia's other recipe is for the Greek cookies she makes during Christmas, called *Kourabiedes*, which are similar to the powdered-sugar pecan balls that have many names, though the Greek version is much lighter.

Greek charm

Vasilopita

Vasilopita (Lucky New Year Cake)

Serves 8 to 10 or more

NOTE: Plan ahead, as the dried fruit must soak overnight. This recipe calls for an 11-inch springform pan because a springform pan makes it easier to remove the cake from the pan. However, other size pans could be used, although the bake time would need to be adjusted. The cake is best when prepared a day before it is to be served, as the flavors get better with time.

1½ cups mixed dried fruit (raisins, prunes, figs, apricots, etc.), plus more for decoration

1 cup brandy or orange juice

2 cups all-purpose flour

1 teaspoon baking powder

1 cup (2 sticks) butter, at room temperature, plus extra for the pan

1½ cups powdered sugar, plus more for decoration

2 cups almond flour

1 teaspoon vanilla extract

6 eggs

In a small bowl, combine the dried fruits and the brandy (or orange juice) and soak the fruit overnight, at room temperature.

The next day, transfer the fruit and its remaining liquid to a blender and process until the mixture becomes a pulp.

Preheat the oven to 350°F. Line the base of an 11-inch round springform pan with parchment paper and grease the bottom and sides with butter.

In a medium bowl, whisk together the all-purpose flour and baking powder, and set aside.

Beat the butter and powdered sugar in the bowl of an electric mixer on medium-high speed until creamy, about 2 minutes. Slowly add the almond flour, beating until the mixture is smooth. Add the fruit pulp and vanilla extract and continue to beat for 1 to 2 minutes. Reduce the speed to low and add the eggs, one at a time, mixing well after each addition. Use a spatula to fold the flour mixture into the egg mixture. The batter will be thick.

Pour the batter into the prepared springform pan and smooth the top with a spatula. Bake until a toothpick or fork inserted into the cake comes out clean, 45 to 60 minutes. Remove the cake from the oven and set it on a wire rack to cool to room temperature.

If hiding a coin inside, as Tenia does, take the baked cake out of the pan and place it upside down on a plate. Wrap the coin in aluminum foil and push it into the cake. Flip the cake over (so the top is again on top). Sprinkle with powdered sugar and additional dried fruit. And Tenia reminds the baker to be sure to have a lucky charm for the person who finds the coin in their slice of cake.

Kourabiedes (Greek Christmas Cookies)

Makes about 4 dozen

¾ cup whole or blanched almonds

1¼ cups (2½ sticks) butter, at room temperature

1 cup powdered sugar, plus extra to dust the cookies

¼ cup brandy, rum, or almond liqueur (such as Amaretto)

2½ cups flour

½ teaspoon baking powder

1 pinch salt

Preheat the oven to 350°F. Line the baking sheets with parchment paper.

To toast the almonds, place the nuts in a dry skillet over medium heat and cook, stirring or shaking the skillet frequently, until they just begin to release their fragrance, about 3 to 4 minutes. Remove the skillet from the heat, cool completely, and coarsely chop.

Beat the butter and powdered sugar in the bowl of an electric mixer at low speed for 1 minute. Increase the speed to high and beat until the mixture is fluffy and white, at least 10 minutes. Reduce the speed to low and add the brandy (or rum or liqueur), flour, baking powder, and salt, mixing until combined. Stir in the almond pieces. Once the ingredients are well combined, mix further with your hands until the dough comes together.

Roll the cookie dough into 1-inch balls (about 1 tablespoon of dough per ball) and place them about 2 inches apart on the prepared baking sheet. Lightly press the center of each cookie with your finger (to catch the powdered sugar later) and bake until the bottoms of the cookies are lightly browned, 15 to 20 minutes (the cookies should stay light in color). Remove the cookies from the oven and allow them to cool completely on the baking sheets, preferably overnight.

Immediately before serving, dust the cookies with powdered sugar. Store the remaining cookies, without the powdered sugar, in an airtight container at room temperature. When ready to serve, dust them with powdered sugar.

Kourabiedes

YAN MO
CHINA

Yan Mo was born in Bengbu, China, a city of 3.3 million people. He attended university in Tianjin and earned a master's degree in Wuxi, where he focused on industrial design. In 2013, pursuing his passion, he moved to New York City for a second master's degree at New York University, where he studied interaction technology and user-experience design in the city that's a hub for this industry. Yan now works in user-experience design and lives in Minnesota with his husband, who works with the Advocates for Human Rights.

What reminds Yan of home? The Chinese New Year, steeped in tradition and cultural influences. The celebration is one of the most important in China, one that ushers out the old year and welcomes the new year with hope for health and prosperity. Yan celebrates this occasion with Eight-Treasure Rice Cake, a recipe he describes as "sweet, delicious, and very pretty looking." It's also full of memories. His family makes this recipe only once annually, to celebrate the occasion. The designation of "eight" is symbolic, as the number represents fortune in Chinese culture. The rice cake completes the yearly feast, bringing with it wishes for good fortune to the family for the next year.

In the past, Yan's grandmother made the cake, taking care to do so perfectly. Traditionally, food preparation for this feast was precise because a mistake could invite misfortune in the coming year. He recalls how his grandmother trusted him to place decorations on the cake, making him a part of the preparation. For Yan, food is a constant reminder of home. Having spent most of his life in China, he continues to cook the traditional foods. "Cooking food is healthier and gives myself a sense of homey feeling and also makes other people around me happy," he says. "That's why I like cooking."

Since moving to the United States, Yan has encountered a vast diversity of food cultures from around the world, especially during his time in New York City. He has found that food serves as an important way to learn about and relate to other cultures. "I want people to be more adventurous eaters," he says. "Before you say, 'I won't eat that,' better to try to learn why people eat that way and what is the motivation for that. There is a whole story and historical facts behind why people eat certain things." No need to wait for the Chinese New Year to make Eight-Treasure Rice Cake. *Gong xi fa cai*! Congratulations and be prosperous!

Eight-Treasure Rice Cake

Serves 8

NOTE: Plan ahead, as the rice needs to be soaked for 1 to 2 hours in advance. Goji berries are sold dried in a packet like raisins. You can also add ¼ cup (50 grams) of purple rice into the glutinous rice to make a purple-rice cake version.

- 1¾ cups sweet rice (also called glutinous or sweet glutinous rice)
- ⅓ cup walnuts (or any other unsalted nuts you prefer), chopped, plus ¼ cup nut halves for decoration
- 2 tablespoons sesame seeds, plus more for decoration
- 1 (120-gram) can sweetened red bean paste (also called *anko*)
- ¼ cup chopped dried dates, plus more whole dates for decoration
- ¼ cup dried fruit, chopped (pineapple gives a nice tart flavor), plus more for decoration
- 2 tablespoons raisins, plus more for decoration
- 2 tablespoons goji berries
- ¼ teaspoon salt
- 2 tablespoons shortening or vegetable oil
- 3 tablespoons granulated sugar
- Cooking spray

TO PREPARE THE RICE: Soak the rice in 1½ cups water for 1 to 2 hours, then strain it.

Place the rice and 1½ cups fresh water in a round glass bowl that is heat-safe, such as Pyrex. Place the bowl inside a wok or a pot with a steamer basket that can be removed, deep enough that you can fit a cover on top. Place the cover on and bring the water to a boil. When the water boils, turn the heat to medium and keep steaming the rice for 30 to 40 minutes until the rice is cooked. Glutinous rice will be a bit shiny when it is fully cooked.

TO PREPARE FILLING: While the rice is cooking, toast the chopped nuts in a dry pan over low heat until just turning brown, about 3 to 4 minutes. Toast the sesame seeds in the same way, separately. In a medium bowl, mix the red bean paste with the chopped nuts, sesame seeds, chopped dates and dried fruit, raisins, goji berries, and salt. Knead the mixture into a ball. When the rice is steamed, carefully remove the bowl from the pot, using oven mitts and tongs if needed, and set on a trivet or heat-safe surface. Add the shortening (or vegetable oil) and the sugar to the cooked rice and mix well while the rice is hot.

TO ASSEMBLE: Coat a 7- or 8-inch heat-safe bowl (a flat-bottomed Pyrex bowl works great) with cooking spray. Sprinkle the bottom of the bowl with the ingredients for decoration: dried fruits, nuts and sesame seeds. These will be on top of the rice cake when it is done and inverted. Place most of the rice on top of the decorations and use a spoon to even it out. Then press the rice toward the sides, making a well in the center. Press the filling into the well.

Place the rest of the rice on top of the filling and use the spoon to press it down to seal the filling inside. Do not worry if there are some bare spots but cover as best you can.

Eight-Treasure Rice Cake

Replenish the water in the steaming pot or wok, as needed. Place the bowl with the rice cake back into the steamer pot or wok and cover. Repeat the steaming process for another 30 minutes or more.

Remove the bowl carefully from the pot and place it on a small heat-safe cutting board. Put your serving plate face down on top of the bowl. Hold the board, bowl, and plate together and carefully flip the whole thing over. Slowly and carefully lift the rice cake bowl until the rice cake drops onto the serving plate. If it is not coming down, let gravity do its work, tapping the bowl if needed. Serve at room temperature.

ACKNOWLEDGMENTS

It takes a village to write a book, and for us, the village encompassed the whole world, from Afghanistan to Zimbabwe. Our sincerest thanks to the participants, who spoke from their hearts and who invited us into their lives and kitchens. What a gift and a responsibility, one we took seriously. We hope we lived up to their expectations.

Our gratitude extends to the Advocates for Human Rights and the work this organization has done for more than four decades. We appreciate the advice and counsel provided by all during the three years of this undertaking, especially to the staff who contributed to the book, too many to name here.

A big project requires big support and Faegre Drinker Biddle & Reath LLP stepped in with financial, technical, and clerical assistance, while continuing to be a longtime supporter of the Advocates. Special thanks in particular to Barb Nallick and Darcy Boehme, who prepared countless revisions and helped us manage the content online.

A big hug to our photographer, Tom Wallace, whose attention to and patience for the visual images of the participants and their food transformed the look of the book.

We are grateful to Erik Anderson, senior editor at the University of Minnesota Press, for his careful eye and full-fledged support when we brought the idea of this book to him. Kelly Doudna and Layne Halvorsen of Mighty Media turned all the varied elements into a beautiful book.

On a global note, let us not forget the farmers who feed the world. We are particularly indebted to those who grow the rice and raise the chickens that are significant ingredients for many of the recipes in this book.

On a personal note:

Linda Svitak: It is rare to have the opportunity to share a special project with your sister. This was one of those moments. I am grateful that Lee generously contributed her many talents, from creativity and food styling to editing and process. We could not have completed this book without her. And Christin, my friend and former law partner, is always a joy to work with, as is Tom Wallace, photographer extraordinaire. But the unsung hero is my husband, David Feroe, a great home cook whose support was unwavering from the start. He read and provided feedback on many stories, but perhaps his greatest contributions were seen in the kitchen and at the table, where he tested and tasted many recipes from around the world.

Christin Jaye Eaton: I have been blessed by the laughter, wisdom, and welcome extended by Linda, Lee, and Tom as we worked alongside one another on this adventure. I stand in the midst of a long line of cooks, inspired and supported by my parents and their parents, by my children and their families. I am thankful to the Lord for more miracles than I can count, and to my amazing family and friends for so many hours spent cooking, side by side. By opening their hopes, their lives, and their kitchens, our participants have left us carrying treasure.

Lee Svitak Dean: Sometimes it pays to say "yes." I am grateful that my sister invited me into this cookbook undertaking and for the delightful collaboration with Christin. I appreciate the insight, skill, and friendship of Tom Wallace, my go-to photographer, as well as his calm response to frantic phone calls that start with "We just need one more photo." My thanks to Rick Nelson, my friend and coauthor on other book projects, who lent his discerning eye to the recipes. Most of all, my thanks to the book's participants, who opened my eyes to issues of immigration that never make the evening news. This country is a better place because of them. And it's certainly one with better food.

RESOURCES

SPECIALTY INGREDIENTS

These specialty ingredients are available online and in local markets that cater to a particular global region or nationality.

ají amarillo: A specific Peruvian pepper, aromatic and moderately spicy, and critical to Peruvian cooking; used in a paste.

ají panca: A mild Peruvian pepper grown in Peru and used in Peruvian cuisine; used in a paste.

bò viên meatballs: A chewy style of Vietnamese meatball, available at many Asian markets.

cargamanto bean: Also called a cranberry bean. Originally from Colombia.

cassava: A starchy tuber and a major source of carbohydrates, generally consumed in a boiled form or grated, dried, and roasted into a flour.

culantro (*ngo gai*): A leafy herb that has a similar aroma and flavor as cilantro, although more potent.

epazote: A leafy herb, used in Mexican food, with a strong taste and aroma.

fufu: A dough-like food commonly eaten in many African countries that can be made from mashed cassava or yams that have been boiled, pounded, and shaped into a mound or small balls. Variations include semolina or yam flour for the main ingredient.

garam masala: A blend of many spices frequently used in Indian foods.

ghee: Clarified butter, often used in Indian food.

Hmong chicken soup herbs: A specific variety of fresh herbs traditionally used for a soup served as a post-natal meal for Hmong mothers; available in Hmong markets.

Hmong mustard greens: A specific mustard green available at Hmong grocery stores and many farmers markets, with a different flavor than the more common mustard greens in supermarkets.

jeera seeds: Cumin seeds, used in Indian, Mexican, and Moroccan dishes.

kaymak: A Turkish dairy product, similar to clotted cream.

kefir: A fermented milk similar to a thin yogurt.

kitily: A type of eggplant native to West Africa.

lal mirch: An Indian red chile pepper found at Indian grocery stores. It should not be confused with other chile peppers.

Maggi seasoning: Often used in Asian and African cooking, it comes in liquid, cube, and powdered forms. It provides an umami flavor to foods.

naan: A type of Indian flatbread.

palava leaves: Jute leaves.

pepitas: Hulled green pumpkin seeds, sold either roasted or raw.

plantain: A tropical fruit similar to a banana, but tougher and starchier. When ripe, it is sweeter.

red bean paste: A paste made of red beans used in Asian cooking.

rock sugar: A type of hard sugar about the size of a sugar cube, often available at Asian grocery stores.

star anise: A star-shaped pod used as a spice, with a flavor more bitter than regular anise seed.

tamarind: A tropical fruit grown on a tree that produces bean-like pods that contain seeds and a fibrous pulp. As the seeds ripen, the pulp becomes a paste that is used as a seasoning. Available at Indian grocery stores.

timur: A Himalayan black peppercorn with a citrusy flavor and mouth-tingling properties. Also sold as timut (its French name). Sichuan peppercorns have similar properties.

tomatillo: A small, firm, round green fruit that looks a bit like a green tomato. It's a staple of Mexican cooking.

Turkish flour: The gluten content of this flour makes it stretchable, well-suited to Bosnian pita or phyllo dough. One brand of this flour is Pravi Zlatni Puder, which is available online and at the local Bosnian market.

Vegeta: An all-purpose seasoning that boosts flavor with dehydrated vegetables.

INTERNATIONAL MARKETS

The secret to many of these recipes is the right ingredients. For Minnesota cooks in the Twin Cities, these specialty markets will carry the items you need, particularly the fresh ingredients some recipes recommend. You also can find most of these ingredients online, including spices at penzeys.com and worldmarket.com.

Andale Taqueria y Mercado, 7700 Nicollet Avenue South, Richfield

African International Market, 7617 Welcome Avenue North, Brooklyn Park

Asia Mall, 12160 Technology Drive, Eden Prairie

Bill's Imported Foods, 721 West Lake Street, Minneapolis

Bodega 42 Fresh Market (Mexican and south-of-border), 6999 152nd Street West, Apple Valley

Bosnian Supermarket, 764 County Highway 10, Blaine

Caspian Bistro and Gourmet Marketplace (Persian, Iranian, and halal meat), 2418 University Avenue SE, Minneapolis

Centromex Supermercado (Colombian), 816 East Seventh Street, St. Paul

Colonial Market and Restaurant, 2750 Nicollet Avenue South, Minneapolis

Dong Yang Oriental Foods, 725 45th Avenue NE, Hilltop

Dragon Star Oriental Foods, 633 Minnehaha Avenue West, St. Paul

Dragon Star Supermarket (Asian, African, Indian, and Middle Eastern foods), 8020 Brooklyn Boulevard, Brooklyn Park

El Burrito Mercado, 175 Cesar Chavez Street, St. Paul

Fresh India Grocery and Eatery, 441 Commerce Drive, Woodbury

Golden Harvest Foods (Asian), 900 Maryland Avenue East, St. Paul

Ha Tien Super Market, 1959 Suburban Avenue, St. Paul

Holy Land, 2513 Central Avenue NE, Minneapolis

Hmongtown Marketplace, 217 Como Avenue, Suite 2–100, St. Paul

Hmong Village, 1001 Johnson Parkway, St. Paul

Ingebretsen's Scandinavian Gifts and Foods, 1601 East Lake Street, Minneapolis

Jerusalem Halal Market, 4945 Central Avenue NE, Columbia Heights

Karmel Mall (Somali), 2910 Pleasant Avenue, Minneapolis

Little India International Market, 1835 Central Avenue NE, Minneapolis

Mercado Central, 1515 East Lake Street, Minneapolis

Midtown Global Market, 920 East Lake Street, Minneapolis

Mill City Farmers Market, 750 South Second Street, Minneapolis

Minneapolis Farmers Market, 312 E. Lyndale Avenue North, Minneapolis

Minsk Market (Eastern European), 3920 Cedar Grove Parkway, Eagan

Penzeys Spices, 3028 Hennepin Avenue S., Minneapolis; 674 Grand Avenue, St. Paul

Pooja Grocers, 4864 Central Avenue NE, Hilltop

Saint Paul Farmers Market, 290 East Fifth Street, St. Paul

Sambusa Halal (African grocery), 126 Blake Road North, Hopkins

Shuang Hur, 654 University Avenue West, St. Paul; 2712 Nicollet Avenue, Minneapolis

Sun Foods (Asian), 544 West University Avenue, St. Paul; 6350 Brooklyn Boulevard, Brooklyn Center

United Noodles (Asian and more), 2015 East 24th Street, Minneapolis; 7730 Hudson Road, Suite 60, Woodbury

Viet-Hoa-Lao, 1964 Rahncliff Court, #350, Eagan

Waterside Market (African), 7500 Brooklyn Boulevard, Brooklyn Park

Workinesh Spice Blends (sells farina flour and spices from many countries, including Ethiopia), 3451 Burnsville Parkway, #102, Burnsville

FOR FURTHER READING

Immigration serves as the focal point of many books, from memoir and nonfiction to fiction, cookbooks, poetry, and children's literature.

MEMOIRS

Bastianich, Lidia Matticchio. *My American Dream: A Life of Love, Family, and Food* (Italy)

Beah, Ishmael. *A Long Way Gone: Memoirs of A Boy Soldier* (Sierra Leone)

Bijan, Donia. *Maman's Homesick Pie: A Persian Heart in an American Kitchen* (Iran)

Daniel, Mary-Alice. *A Coastline is an Immeasurable Thing: A memoir across three continents* (Nigeria and U.K.)

Lakshmi, Padma. *Love, Loss, and What We Ate* (India)

Nguon, Chantha. *Slow Noodles: A Cambodian Memoir of Love, Loss, and Family Recipes* (Cambodia, Vietnam, Thailand)

Pépin, Jacques. *The Apprentice: My Life in the Kitchen* (France)

Samuelsson, Marcus. *Yes, Chef: A Memoir* (Ethiopia and Sweden)

Shin, Sun Yung, editor. *What We Hunger For: Refugee and Immigrant Stories about Food and Family*

Von Bremzen, Anya. *Mastering the Art of Soviet Cooking: A Memoir of Food and Longing* (Soviet Union)

Wang, Qian Julie. *A Beautiful Country: A Memoir of an Undocumented Childhood* (China)

Yang, Kao Kalia. *The Latehomecomer: A Hmong Family Memoir* (Hmong)

Yang, Kao Kalia. *The Song Poet: A Memoir of My Father* (Hmong)

Yang, Kao Kalia. *Somewhere in the Unknown World: A Collective Refugee Memoir* (Hmong)

Yang, Kao Kalia. *Where Rivers Part: A Story of My Mother's Life* (Hmong)

Zamora, Javier. *Solito: A Memoir* (El Salvador)

Zauner, Michelle. *Crying in H Mart* (Korea)

COOKBOOKS

The Eat Offbeat Chefs. *The Kitchen without Borders: Recipes and Stories from Refugee and Immigrant Chefs*

Gass, Anna Francese, and Andrew Scrivani. *Heirloom Kitchen: Heritage Recipes and Family Stories from the Tables of Immigrant Women*

Harris, Phyllis Louise, with Raghavan Iver. *Asian Flavors: Changing the Tastes of Minnesota since 1875*

Hassan, Hawa, with Julia Turshen. *In Bibi's Kitchen: The Recipes and Stories of Grandmothers from the Eight African Countries That Touch the Indian Ocean*

Refugee Women's Alliance. *Recipes for Refuge: Culinary Journeys to America*

Richmond, Ann. *Food for Thought: A World of Flavor and Perspective from Idaho's Refugees and Friends*

NONFICTION

Amrhein, Saundra, and Ariana Lindquist. *Green Card Stories*

Blitzer, Jonathan. *Everyone Who Is Gone Is Here: The United States, Central America, and the Making of a Crisis*

Fadiman, Anne. *The Spirit Catches You and You Fall Down* (Hmong)

Goudeau, Jessica. *After the Last Border: Two Families and the Story of Refuge in America* (Myanmar and Syria)

King, Michelle T. *Chop Fry Watch Learn: Fu Pei-Mei and the Making of Modern Chinese Food* (Taiwan and China)

Lee, Edward. *Buttermilk Graffiti: A Chef's Journey to Discover America's New Melting-Pot Cuisine*

Lee, Jennifer 8. *The Fortune Cookie Chronicles: Adventures in the World of Chinese Food*

Nayeri, Dina. *The Ungrateful Refugee: What Immigrants Never Tell You* (Iran)

Nazario, Sonia. *Enrique's Journey* (Honduras)

Sen, Mayukh. *Tastemakers: Seven Immigrant Women Who Revolutionized Food in America* (China, France, India, Iran, Italy, Jamaica, and Mexico)

Soni, Saket. *The Great Escape: A True Story of Forced Labor and Immigrant Dreams in America* (India)

Ying, Chris, editor. *You and I Eat the Same: On the Countless Ways Food and Cooking Connect Us to One Another* (collection of essays)

FICTION

Alvarez, Julia. *How the García Girls Lost Their Accents* (Dominican Republic)

Bijan, Donia. *The Last Days of Café Leila* (Iran)

Cather, Willa. *My Ántonia* (Bohemia)

Eggers, Dave. *What Is the What: The Autobiography of Valentino Achak Deng* (Sudan)

Garcia, Gabriela. *Of Women and Salt* (Cuba)

Kwok, Jean. *Girl in Translation* (Hong Kong)

Lahiri, Jhumpa. *The Namesake* (India)

Rolvaag, Ole. *Giants in the Earth* (Norway)

Tan, Amy. *Joy Luck Club* (China)

Toossi, Sanaz. *English* (a play) (Iran)

PICTURE BOOKS

Eggers, Dave, with illustrations by Shawn Harris. *Her Right Foot* (United States)

Lakshmi, Padma, with illustrations by Juana Martinez-Neal. *Tomatoes for Neela* (India)

Martinez-Neal, Juana. *Alma, and How She Got Her Name* (Peru)

Mora, Pat, with illustrations by Raúl Colón. *Tomás and the Library Lady* (Mexican American)

Polacco, Patricia. *Fiona's Lace* (Ireland)

Tan, Shaun. *The Arrival* (Universal)

Yang, Kao Kalia, with illustrations by Rachel Wada. *From the Tops of Trees* (Hmong)

Yang, Kao Kalia, with illustrations by Khoa Le. *The Most Beautiful Thing* (Hmong)

Wang, Andrea, with illustrations by Jason Chin. *Watercress* (China)

YOUTH

Engle, Margarita. *Enchanted Air: Two Cultures, Two Wings* (Cuba)

Johnston, Tony. *Any Small Goodness* (Mexico)

Lai, Thanhha. *Inside Out & Back Again* (Vietnam)

Pinkney, Andrea David, with illustrations by Shane W. Evans. *The Red Pencil* (Sudan)

Ryan, Pam Muñoz. *Esperanza Rising* (Mexico)

Warga, Jasmine. *Other Words for Home* (Syria)

Yang, Gene Luen. *American Born Chinese* (Chinese American)

POETRY

Keenan, Deborah and Roseann Lloyd, editors. *Looking for Home: Women Writing about Exile*

Nye, Naomi Shihab. *Words under the Words* (Palestinian American)

Vecchione, Patrice, and Alyssa Raymond, editors. *Ink Knows No Borders: Poems of the Immigrant and Refugee Experience*

Vuong, Ocean. *Night Sky with Exit Wounds* (Vietnam)

INDEX

APPETIZERS AND BEVERAGES

SAUCES

BREAD, GRAINS, AND LEGUMES

SOUPS

VEGETABLES AND SALADS

VEGETARIAN MAIN DISHES

MEAT, POULTRY, AND FISH

SWEETS AND DESSERTS

LINDA S. SVITAK was a trial lawyer at Faegre Drinker Biddle & Reath in Minneapolis for thirty-five years. She has long been committed to pro bono service, particularly in women's, children's, and international human rights. For more than a decade, she has volunteered with the Advocates for Human Rights and has participated in advocacy at the United Nations in Geneva, Switzerland, including delivering an oral statement on the floor at the Human Rights Council of the United Nations.

CHRISTIN JAYE EATON has served as science counsel in lawsuits involving many different products and chemicals, which has been a highlight in her thirty years practicing law with Faegre Drinker Biddle & Reath (and its predecessors) in Minneapolis. Her pro bono service has included cases involving immigrant status, and she was introduced to the Advocates for Human Rights through its collaborations with her law firm.

LEE SVITAK DEAN spent four decades writing about food for the *Star Tribune* in Minneapolis, including twenty-six years as editor of the Taste section. She and her staff won four James Beard awards. She is coauthor of the cookbooks *The Great Minnesota Cookie Book* and *The Ultimate Minnesota Cookie Book* from the University of Minnesota Press, as well as author of *Come One, Come All: Easy Entertaining with Seasonal Recipes*. She was a member of the James Beard Foundation Book Awards committee for more than a decade.

TOM WALLACE had an award-winning career in small-town community journalism before arriving at the *Star Tribune* as a photographer and photo editor. He has received national recognition for his work.

LOAN HUYNH has practiced immigration law for more than twenty years. She chairs the immigration department at the law firm Fredrikson & Byron in Minneapolis, as well as serving on its Diversity and Inclusion Committee. From 1996 until 1999, she was an attorney at the Advocates for Human Rights in its Refugee Immigrant Program, and she has served on its board. She fled Vietnam in 1975 with her siblings and parents.